Andy Warhol's
Ridiculous Screenplays

Andy Warhol's
Ridiculous Screenplays
by Ronald Tavel

FAST BOOKS

Publication of this book was made possible by the generous support of Norman R. Glick and the Estate of Norman R. Glick.

Most of the Tavel/Warhol films, withdrawn from circulation in the early 1970s, have been restored and are available for viewing through the Museum of Modern Art in New York. Facsimile manuscripts of Ronald Tavel's screenplays can be found at ronaldtavel.com, where these texts first appeared in a different form.

On the cover: Ronald Tavel during the writing of *Tarzan of the Flicks,* 1962, photograph by Harvey Tavel; Andy Warhol filming, photograph by Billy Name.

Fast Books are edited and published by Michael Smith, P. O. Box 1268, Silverton, Oregon 97381

ISBN 978-0-9887162-9-2

Mon verre n'est pas grand.
Mais je ne bois pas dans mon verre.

Contents

Ridiculous Screenplays

Marc Siegel

Surely the most ridiculous thing about Andy Warhol's screenplays is that they exist at all. Popular opinion about Warhol's films tells us that he just pushed a button and left, leaving alone those in front of the camera to decide what to do and—in the case of the sound films—what to say. With his own statements, Warhol fostered such misconceptions about his work, encouraging people to think that he only turned to film because it was easier than painting and that his films were better talked about than seen.

Whether taken as automatic machinic reproductions of reality or conceptual thought experiments, Warhol's films seem to defy the idea of an originating screenplay. Perhaps there were notes, instructions, or guidelines. But dialogue-driven, narratively and dramatically structured screenplays? That seems unlikely—ridiculous, even. Moreover, when Warhol shifted from minimalist silent films to performance-oriented sound features, he turned his camera onto the improvisational antics of a group of often drunk and drugged-out Factory Superstars. How could these distracted and untrained performers be expected to follow the intricacies of a preconceived script? What kind of writer would have agreed to hone his chops at dramatic writing in such an inhospitable milieu?

Andy Warhol's Ridiculous Screenplays is a fascinating first-person account of writer Ronald Tavel's experiences collaborating with the artist on his films from the winter of 1964 through the summer of 1967. During this period, Tavel wrote seventeen screenplays for Warhol, including some of the most significant works in the artist's filmography and in American underground film more broadly: *Screen Test #2, The Life of Juanita Castro, Horse, Vinyl, Kitchen* (all 1965), *Hedy*, and two sections of *The Chelsea Girls* (both 1966). The nature of filmmaking in Warhol's Silver Factory of the mid-1960s meant that Tavel's role as screenwriter was not restricted to a film's pre-production. In most cases, he was responsible as well for directing, performing, and facilitating the performance of the screenplays during filming itself. This is most obvious in his performances as the off-screen voice of the "Tester" in *Screen Test #1* and *Screen Test #2* and the on-screen "Director" in *The Life of Juanita Castro*. But Tavel's distinctive Brooklyn accent is familiar to many a viewer from the soundtracks to a number of other Warhol films as well, including the artist's first sound film, *Harlot* (1964), in which Tavel animates a lively and innuendo-ridden off-screen discussion with Factory regular Billy Name and poet Harry Fainlight.

Tavel was one of the few people who worked closely and consistently with Warhol on the conception and realization of his early sound films, and he is therefore perfectly poised to shed insight into the artist's filmmaking process. This book, therefore, offers both the story of Tavel's screenplays and a powerful revelation about his artistic collaboration with Warhol in the 1960s, a complicated working relationship that art historian Douglas Crimp has described as "one of the most productive artistic collaborations in the recent history of the avant-garde."

When Warhol met him in the fall of 1964, Ronald Tavel was a poet and novelist in his late twenties. With a master's degree in creative writing from the University of Wyoming and a couple of publications behind him, the young writer took part in readings at various venues in Lower Manhattan while he shopped around an 813-page manuscript for a novel called *Street of Stairs*, based on his travels in North Africa. (The novel was eventually published in 1968, in abridged form, by Olympia Press.) Along with his poems, which he produced on a weekly rhythm, Tavel was likely to have been reading excerpts from *Street of Stairs* on the November evening when poet Gerard Malanga took Warhol to hear him at the Café le Metro. Impressed by the sound of Tavel's voice, his talent, and his seemingly prolific output, Warhol invited him to the Factory to supply the soundtrack for his first sound film, *Harlot*. He was expected to read from his novel, poems, "or maybe the telephone directory." At the outset of the film shoot shortly thereafter, Warhol initiated what would be the first of many a "last-minute turnabout intended to dismantle a performance possibly prepared in advance—along with the fictions of a rehearsed performance." He asked Tavel instead to carry on a spontaneous conversation with Name and Fainlight.

So began an unexpectedly fruitful—Tavel terms it a "lateral"—collaboration based on minimal, mumbling communication, sideways glances, and last-minute changes. It seemed destined not to last, which was fine for Tavel, a trained writer whose main interest lay in publishing his novel and not in writing the screenplays that he nevertheless churned out at an astounding rate. Over a seven-month period, from January to July 1965, Tavel wrote the bulk of his most celebrated Warhol screenplays, eleven works in all, from *Screen Test #1* and *#2* through *Juanita Castro, Vinyl*, and a never-filmed script for a Hawaiian surfer movie called *Kahuna!* He developed a means of discerning Warhol's interests and ingeniously inventing ever-new solutions to the problems posed by Factory filmmaking. Faced with the fact that Warhol didn't usually allow rehearsals and that most performers couldn't or wouldn't memorize anything in advance (if they were even allowed to see the script), Tavel took on the role of off-screen voice soliciting on-screen responses (the *Screen Test* features, *Suicide*); created the character of "Director" to read each line in advance of the performers (*Juanita Castro*); hid the script on the set in case the performers forgot their lines (*Kitchen*); created enormous idiot boards to prompt from off-screen (*Vinyl, Horse*); conceived situations and sequences that allowed improvisational leeway (*Kitchen, Hedy*); and supplied dialogue lists organized according to the *I Ching* and intended for random use by alternating performers (*Space*). Warhol required a new conceptual approach to each film, and Tavel dutifully responded in suit. Critics began to take the work seriously—*Village Voice* film critic Andrew Sarris singled out the writer for *The Life of Juanita Castro*—and Tavel finally began to recognize the value of his film work.

For little more than half a year, Tavel was an indispensable fixture of Warhol's filmmaking enterprises, his resident scenarist. While mixing with the uptown debutantes and slumming socialites in the artist's midtown Factory, Tavel maintained close relations to the Lower Manhattan artistic subculture that had initially nurtured his creative energies. Before meeting Warhol, he was involved in the broader cultural scene around filmmaker and artist Jack Smith. He appeared in Smith's photo shoots, worked on his legendary 1962 film *Flaming Creatures*, and shared with Smith a highly generative obsession with Hollywood films of the 1930s and '40s, particularly those like *Arabian Nights* (John Rawlins, 1942) and *Cobra Woman* (Robert Siodmak, 1944) that featured the Queen of Technicolor, Maria Montez. "The importance of Smith for me," Tavel claimed, "is that he said, 'Don't forget your childhood. Exploit it… Take all the childhood fears, anxieties, impressions, loves, and all of that and use that for art.'" Through his work and friendship with Smith—which lasted until the latter's death in 1989—Tavel learned to move beyond his training in classical literature and bring his childhood love of Hollywood movies and popular culture to bear on his creative work. His affective investment in Hollywood manifests itself in his work not only in the many references to movie stars, genre films, and film dialogue, but also in the dramatic intensity and emotional inflection of his writing. Smith wanted Tavel to aspire to the sensibility of an escapist Technicolor Montez film, "romantic and lush and Arabian, purples and reds and all of that." Warhol, on the other hand, restricted Tavel's fantasies to "black and white and New York City. If you hate New York I want to see that hatred." One ridiculous aspect of Tavel's work, therefore, can likely be traced back to a condensation of these distinctively opposing aesthetic sensibilities.

In Tavel's florid narration about the tensions between these two key figures in his artistic development, Smith and Warhol function alternately as warring Hollywood studio bosses and rival Caliphs at battle for his loyalty and artistic talents. Interestingly, he attributes his eventual departure from the Factory to the "Smith/Tavel/Warhol interdynamic." Things apparently came to a head with Warhol in May 1965 during the rehearsal period for *Kitchen*, when Tavel was writing intertitles for an unfinished early Smith film, a riff on Montez's *Arabian Nights* called *Buzzards over Baghdad*. This side work didn't escape Warhol's attention, and Tavel received the artist's disarming acknowledgement of it as a sign of "territory-marking." "I was tongue-tied," he writes, "and uncontrollably accepted his obloquy of my moonlighting as artistic treachery." Describing this incident with the same melodramatic flair he would accord a disastrous plot twist in a Montez film, Tavel retrospectively judges this collaboration with Smith as a fatal act of insubordination that would irreparably alter his working relationship with Warhol—"the rare and enviable imperative among us would never after be the same."

Most accounts of Tavel's break with Warhol, however, highlight instead a tension with one of the Factory's other social and artistic scenes, namely the one that circulated around Edie Sedgwick. The iconic, doomed underground glamor girl made her first brief screen appearances in Warhol's Tavel films *Bitch, Horse,* and *Vinyl* before becoming the star of a series of improvisational films about her daily and romantic life, *Beauty #1, Beauty #2,* and *Poor Little Rich Girl.* Between March and June 1965, Warhol worked concurrently on the scripted Tavel films and the unscripted Sedgwick ones. Despite her considerable screen magnetism, Sedgwick was not interested in or gifted for learning lines. As Tavel describes it, she became increasingly unstable due to her drug dependencies and, entering a period of hedonism and confusion, agreed to join forces with her friend Chuck Wein in displacing Tavel from Warhol's good graces. Confronted with the script for *Shower,* a new Sedgwick vehicle that Tavel considered his "best work under the painter's tutelage," the star protested to Warhol that she would no longer continue as "a mouthpiece for Tavel's perversities." Warhol stood by Sedgwick but recognized the value of Tavel's new work, suggesting that he stage the script as a theatre piece instead—and connected him with a befriended director to help him on his way.

Despite the Smith/Tavel/Warhol interdynamic and the Tavel/Sedgwick/Wein tensions, the writer nevertheless continued to collaborate with Warhol on his films, contributing, in 1965, screenplays for *Space* (with Sedgwick) and the never-filmed *Kahuna!* In 1966, Tavel followed with *Hedy, Their Town,* and *Hanoi Hannah, Radio Star*— the latter two were filmed and used as segments of the double-screen epic *The Chelsea Girls.* Additionally, at Warhol's request, he penned such little-known screenplays as *Withering Sights, Jane Eyre Bare,* and *Movie Talk for Mary Woronov,* none of which was ever filmed. What changed after the *Shower* incident was thus not the fact but the nature of the Warhol/Tavel collaboration. With *Hedy,* for instance, Warhol allowed Tavel greater leeway with the cast, suggesting he bring along his trusted friends and performers to appear alongside Factory regulars like Gerard Malanga and newcomers (Ingrid Superstar, Mary Woronov, and The Velvet Underground). With drag Superstar Mario Montez, Jack Smith, Smith regular Arnold Rockwood, and Tavel's brother Harvey performing key roles, Tavel was guaranteed at least a few sympathetic collaborators who shared his sensibility and respected his script. (Tavel was nevertheless traumatized by the filming of *Hedy,* thanks mainly to Warhol's unpredictable camera movements that seemed attentive to anything other than narrative space. On a positive note, the film represented the start of a productive collaboration with Mary Woronov that carried over into Tavel's work in theatre.) In the case of *The Chelsea Girls,* Tavel for the first time did not participate in the filming and simply sent in his scripts from California, where he was traveling at the time. His final collaboration with Warhol took place in the summer of 1967 when he chanced upon the filming of *Jail* at the Filmmakers' Cinematheque, and the artist spontaneously asked him to supply some improvised dialogue to spice up the onscreen performances.

In telling the story of his screenplays and his almost

three years of collaboration with Warhol, Tavel provides as well a sketch of the diverse figures and conflictual social and artistic scenes in the Factory. But *Andy Warhol's Ridiculous Screenplays* is not just another in the growing series of mythologizing accounts of those crazy drug- and sex-filled years in the 1960s New York underground. Tavel's intentions are too serious for that, and his book remains focused on detailing the nature of his crucial contributions to Warhol's cinema. To this end, he engages throughout with critical and scholarly writing on the films in order to commend or amend it. Although highly illuminating, Tavel's engagement with the reception of Warhol's films at times leaves a slightly bitter aftertaste. For all the genuine respect—even awe—that he feels for Warhol, he seems to have experienced their work together as frustrating and traumatizing, as much as it was energizing and inspiring. The book chronicles their collaboration as a series of disappointments and complaints: neither Warhol nor the performers took the scripts seriously; Warhol's camera worked at cross purposes with the script; Tavel increasingly felt implicated in the humiliation and shaming of the vulnerable Superstars; he wasn't sufficiently remunerated for his work; and the significance of the screenplays has not been adequately acknowledged in the Warhol literature. Writing well over three decades after the end of their collaboration, Tavel remains convinced that he deserved better; hence, the occasional self-aggrandizing gesture. As the story of a neglected Warhol collaborator, Tavel's account thus links up with those by others whose significant contributions have been obscured by the massive proprietary reach of the artist's brand name. That said, it is safe to say that Tavel really hasn't gotten his due, either for his key role as writer of the ingenious and hilarious screenplays that shaped the direction of Warhol's sound films or—I should add—for his significant contributions to American theatre.

Beyond claiming his rightful place in the history of Warhol's filmmaking, Tavel offers tremendous insight into and little-known information about the production context and aesthetics of the films. Warhol's film shoots, he notes with regret, often functioned like semi-public performance actions or "carnival events" attended by a steady flow of photographers, artists, and other curious Factory visitors. Such a context shifted the meaning and dynamics of the performance for the camera. The intimate exchange between Tavel as off-screen voice and Mario Montez as on-screen performer in *Screen Test #2*, for instance, was hardly a private affair. Tavel charts Warhol's evolving decisions about camera movement and placement and reveals some of his unexpected aesthetic ideas. Given the temporal linearity of most of Warhol's films, it's quite surprising to learn, for instance, that there were plans to employ flashbacks in the form of rear-projections for the filming of *Their Town*. In carefully contextualizing his screenplays, in terms of their genesis, their sometimes obscure references, and their position in Warhol's filmography, Tavel brings to light further bits of curious information. For example, he claims that *Jane Eyre* and *Wuthering Heights* were Warhol's favorite novels and therefore served as sources for two of his screenplays. *Hanoi Hannah, Radio Star* was apparently written because Warhol wanted to do something about the Vietnam War: "Gee, everybody's doing something about the war, Ronnie, shouldn't we do something about the war?" The book is also sprinkled with references to sexuality and the gay subcultural dynamics that course through the films. This is perhaps nowhere more evident than in Tavel's powerful account of the making of *Suicide*, a film focused on a closeted

French film star and occasional Factory visitor with a history of unsuccessful sucide attempts written on his wrists: "How crucial some felt it was to cover their minority sexuality in those days could not be more graphic than the living record this movie makes of that."

Whether describing his psychological state when confronted with a last-minute Warhol turnabout or detailing the life story of a forgotten Factory figure, Tavel retains a witty and sprightly tone. Indeed, beyond the many insights and revelations about Warhol's cinema, it is Tavel's inimitable writing style that provides some of the book's greatest pleasures. He is a unique stylist, whose vocabulary incorporates archaic words, references to classical literature and esoteric Hollywood genre films, and frequent puns and double-entendres. Moving fluidly from simple, expository statements to more poetic syntax, and hardly shying away from convoluted or obscure sentences, Tavel clearly relishes the rich and expressive possibilities of language. If the writing occasionally departs from the task of clarity and leaves us alone for a moment to ruminate on its meaning, it never loses a devilish energy that lends even the most opaque prose a kind of strange purpose. Tavel brings a sense of mystery, theatricality, and intensity to the narration of his working experiences with Warhol and is well aware that such overdramatization borders on the ridiculous. In fact, storytelling as heightened, self-referential, somewhat ludicrous, pun- and innuendo-filled drama might be considered a further trait of the "ridiculous" style that Tavel introduced into 1960s screen- and playwriting.

In the summer of 1965, Tavel followed Warhol's advice and took his script for *Shower* to stage director Jerry Benjamin, who referred him further to downtown performer John Vaccaro, a figure associated with Jack Smith through his appearance in *Normal Love* (1963-65). Vaccaro agreed to stage *Shower*, and it was presented on a double bill with Tavel's *The Life of Juanita Castro* at the Coda Gallery in the East Village on July 29, 1965. Tavel and Vaccaro thus gave birth to a new direction in underground theatre: "Theatre of the Ridiculous" as Tavel termed it. Tavel's artistic focus quickly shifted from cinema to theatre, even as he continued—as noted above—to collaborate with Warhol on the occasional film. He began writing new work specifically for the stage, while also revamping previous Warhol screenplays like *Screen Test #2* and *Kitchen* for live theatrical presentations, directed either by Vaccaro or Tavel's brother, Harvey. The Ridiculous gained momentum, garnered some critical and cult success, and eventually split in three directions, with Vaccaro directing work under the auspices of the Play-House of the Ridiculous and newcomer Charles Ludlam writing and directing for the Ridiculous Theatrical Company. For his part, Tavel continued to write plays in a Ridiculous mode that were staged by various directors (for example *Gorilla Queen*, directed by Lawrence Kornfeld at Judson Memorial Church in March 1967). In his playwriting, Tavel branched out from the Ridiculous as well, occasionally dipping back into his repertoire of Warhol screenplays for material to use for more straightforward dramas, such as the socially concerned piece of Americana, *Boy on the Straight-Back Chair*, based on his script for *Their Town*, which won an Obie Award in 1969. Tavel became one of the key Off-Off-Broadway dramatists of the late 1960s and early '70s and went on to write more than forty plays, many of which furthered the themes and developed the styles he honed during his period of collaboration with Warhol. In addition to his plays, Tavel, who died in 2009, published numerous essays, poems, and a second novel, *Chain*, which appeared posthumously (Fast Books, 2012). An entertaining and intelligent raconteur, he was a much-sought-after interviewee by scholars and documentarians attempting to understand the work of Warhol, Smith, and the 1960s underground.

If one of the goals of *Andy Warhol's Ridiculous Screenplays* is to illuminate Tavel's importance for Warhol films, another is to establish definitively—as the programmatic title of the book's appendix puts it—"The Roots of the Theatre of the Ridiculous in the Scripted Films of Andy Warhol." Tavel's challenging scholarly essay revisits and reframes the story of his Warhol collaborations with an eye for those themes, situations, and concepts that fertilized an idea of "The Ridiculous." (In his essay, Tavel capitalizes both words when referring to the singularity of this concept.) He obviously resents the fact that the term has come to describe a range of work that—to his mind—stylistically, thematically, and ethically differs greatly from his own (for example, Vaccaro's later stagings of plays by Kenneth Bernard).

Hovering in the background of Tavel's discontent, moreover, is the fact that Charles Ludlam—who notably receives only an insignificant footnote in the essay—brought the term "ridiculous" a hitherto unheard-of popularity and resonance within the world of theatre through his writings and his three decades of work at the head of the Ridiculous Theatrical Company. Ludlam's career began with his appearances in Tavel's plays. That said, Tavel is definitely not interested in claiming for himself Ludlam's admittedly relevant and complex understanding of The Ridiculous. To the contrary, he would likely argue that Ludlam's work was not Ridiculous at all—at least not according to Tavel's understanding of the term. And it is Tavel's conception of The Ridiculous that his essay attempts to place at the origins of the multi-faceted movement known as the Theatre of the Ridiculous.

I'll leave it to others to work out the distinctions between different concepts of The Ridiculous—certainly a worthy and productive task, but one that demands far more analysis than this introduction warrants. The motivation for Tavel's Ridiculous, however, might well serve adequately as a characterization of what drives each of these theatrical modes: "to center a rage for retaliatory iconoclasm in a series of aggressively deconstructive events." As he elaborates, The Ridiculous should not be reduced to the question of its content alone: an unpredictable hilarity; a questioning of the boundaries betweeen high art and popular culture; a heavy dose of Hollywood references; a challenge to the distinctions between man and woman, and human and animal; and a bawdy sexual transgressiveness, among other things. Tavel's deconstructive Ridiculous is an exercise in form as well, one that employs a language that playfully resists logic and continually doubles back upon upon itself.

One element seems central to Tavel's conception of The Ridiculous, namely, a challenge to the ontological status of the play. "Today," Tavel notes, "Ridiculous companies do 'plays.' I never intended that. They must offer only *they gathering*, for The Ridiculous is a proposal. It proposes, never supposes theatre." One could well imagine that the work with Warhol provided an unexpectedly ideal, if understandably frustrating, training ground for writing scripts that do not suppose but propose. Such Ridiculous screen- and stageplays maintain a fragile existence and may even seem to dissolve into the cinematic or theatrical event, the "they gathering," that the scripts have helped call into being. Their purpose is not to employ dialogue so as to fully determine character, construct drama, and propel situations. As Tavel evocatively puts it in relation to the Warhol screenplays, the task of the script is "to prepare a field, to arrange a comfort in which to allow, elicit, or conjole the emergence of the indismissible."

Surely the most ridiculous thing about Andy Warhol's screenplays is that they exist at all. Tavel's indispensable book makes clear exactly how these screenplays came to be while offering a suggestive rumination on what it is that makes their fragile existence so ridiculous.

References: Douglas Crimp, *"Our Kind of Movie": The Films of Andy Warhol*. Cambridge, MA: MIT, 2012; Matthias Haase and Marc Siegel, "Do It Again! Do It Again! An Interview with Ronald Tavel," *Criticism* 56.2 (2014): 329-359.

Andy Warhol's
Ridiculous Screenplays

Harlot

By the summer of 1964 I was writing a poem every week and reading it that Wednesday night at Le Métro Coffeehouse, a sizable step-down on Second Avenue between Ninth and Tenth Streets. These midweek open readings were considered important events in New York's cultural life back then, and they were very popular. You never knew who might be there, Ginsberg, Corso, Orlovsky—or the local celebs I remember, who tended to be regulars: Szabo, Rochelle Owens, Susan Sherman, Ishmael Reed, Alan Plantz, Wesley Day, Joe Berke, Barbara Holland, Marguerite Harris, John Keys, John Weiners, and Gerard Malanga.

And I remember the queen bees whose carefully scrutinized attendance was socio-political as much as literary. Most formidable amongst these were Carol Bergé and Diane Wakoski, who entered with their corona of gay male drones and sat at separate tables as if in armed, hostile camps. Woe to the drone who arrived in the brace of one encampment and switched tables during the evening. For he who rides a tiger's back, as the Chinese say, must beware the moment of descent. Such a public defection risked a queen bee's molting into a scissor-lady.

One night in November, a queen bee of another (non) color arrived and upped the buzzing about the crowded café by several decibels. It was living legend Andy Warhol and his mysteriously enslaved, fawning drones who'd a talent themselves for turning into (albeit) minor legends. Gerard Malanga, his salaried assistant, had suggested to Mr. Warhol that he might come that night specifically to hear me. Not my poems, but my voice.

Having recently completed a controversial and ground-breaking set of silent films with an unmoved Bolex 8mm camera, notably, *Eat, Sleep, Kiss,* and *Haircut,* the Pop artist had invested in a 16mm sync-sound Auricon, and was quite as fortified as he deemed justified to delve now into talkies. So though he'd continue to approach the medium as a primarily visual, if not outright painterly, affair—a barely breathing, carefully composed painting as it were—he would be adding speech to his films. Nor was he in the least deterred by not knowing what kind of speech. However, in keeping with how he attacked, literally, the accepted visual language of the medium—a study of studied movement as opposed to action—it was human sound itself that interested him at the moment rather than anything actually said.

I had a comment-inducing technique for public readings in those days. I used to deliberately and diabolically caress phrases, adding a rigorous respect for form and the independence of single lines that was almost religious to a dramatic build that seldom deserted me even when I read impromptu, when requested, someone else's poems, as the sonorous A. B. Spellman's. More to the point here, some poetry-reciting aficionados report that my voice was identical to the sound that the Serpent surely had in the Garden of Eden. Immodestly enough, I have to relay this appraisal since it was just that hyperbole that brought Andy Warhol irresistibly to Le Métro: and his concurring with it that prompted his asking me to talk in his first sound film: which arrangement ultimately led to my becoming his screenwriter.

He sent me his card, asked me to come to his table, and, when I did, abruptly said: "Wanna be in movies?

"Doing what?" I inquired.

"Reading onto the soundtrack. Your novel, or your

poetry. Or maybe the telephone directory."

But when I showed for the shooting at the Factory, in a typical last-minute turnabout intended to dismantle a performance possibly prepared in advance—along with the fictions of a rehearsed performance—Andy instructed me to converse instead with British poet Harry Fainlight and the Factory photographer and manager, Billy Linich, later known as Billy Name.

So, sitting on cushions and sharing their bottle of gin, I noted the speech and response patterns of these two fellows, broke the ice with them so to speak, and when the shoot started, directed the colloquy as best I could.

A curtain had been placed between us and the group of five to be filmed in order that whatever we talked about not be related to what was to be seen. But since Andy had undermined the artifice at which I had practice and for which I had steeled myself, it seemed—for the sake of art—only grateful to return the favor. Accordingly, I razored a slit in the curtain, which permitted Harry, Billy, and me to peek through at the proceedings from time to time: because I figured chitchat completely unrelated to what the audience would be watching might prove too obviously abstract and unintentionally dull: and the boys, by then under the influence, had already waxed sufficiently abstract; and sporadically dull.

H*arlot* (try pronouncing that in French) is a commentary on Jean Harlow herself as well as her windfall of mid-sixties screen and book bios. A few students of Underground Film would like to give it a somewhat literal interpretation, claiming that the luxuriously fidgeting tableau of five represents Jean, her husband, her heavy mother, and her mother's lover—with the fluffy Angora (its screen name was

White Pussy, as in *White Cargo* [with Hedy Lamarr], *White Savage* [with Maria Montez], *White Zombie, White Fang,* etc.) characteristically there in order to stare out at the public while the public stares in at the biopic tableau. But that cat was actually scrutinizing the techies and off-screen talkies, and you can tell if there's stirring amongst us by the cat's ear-alert or its pupils' adjustments to the shifting camera lights. And claiming that any Warhol film so literally represents historical persons, other than in this case Jean Harlow, of course, does not feel right to me.

Assuming a gossip-monger's and perpetual toaster's personality on the soundtrack, I myself was truly distracted by the still-frame's classical composition: transvestite René Rivera (screen name, Mario Montez) reclining on the red couch, an upholstered veteran of numerous celluloid opii, next to buxom Carol Koshinsky with White Pussy on her lap, and Gerard Malanga resting his elbows on the back of the couch, occasionally sharing a cigarette with poker-faced Philip Fagan at his side. René removes a number of bananas from his purse, peels and devours them suggestively, White Pussy gets antsy and attempts to escape: and that's about the sum of the seventy minutes' activity. In beautiful black and white, an epic of patience taking patience to watch, it is two reels of dividending thoughtfulness, and I was glued to the web of insidious logic in the Pop King's aesthetic from that day forth.

A ndy knew that Jean Cocteau had published the notes he took while filming *Orphée* in order to promote that film. So he asked me to do something similar, write a diary of the making of *Harlot*, its first screenings, the reaction of the critics and public, and so on. That book-length promotional is called *The Banana Diary*. Andy saw to its immediate publication.

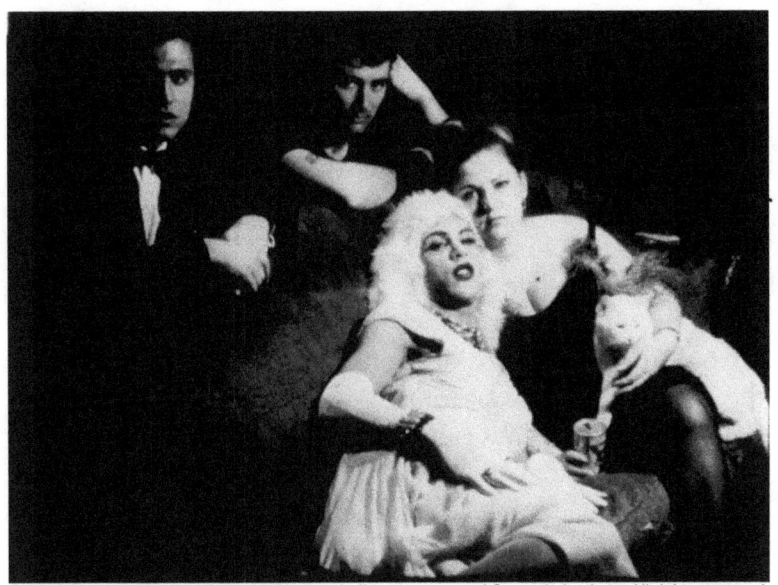

Gerard Malanga, Philip Fagan, Mario Montez, and Carol Koshinsky with White Pussy in Andy Warhol: "Harlot" (1964).

It has since been translated into several languages and most recently reprinted in *Andy Warhol: Film Factory*, edited by Michael O'Pray[1].

In the main, *Harlot* attracted the attention that Andy sought and garnered the accolades he'd hoped for, though the most enthusiastic praise rarely matches what the majority of artists think they deserve. But since its noisy premiere, and for no particular reason, this careful study has received scant examination. And so its beauties, by and large, remain unexplored.

---

1 London: British Film Institute, 1989; Indiana University Press, 1990.

At the time I joined his inner circle Andy was already well-known, and that notoriety had been achieved in part through the most expeditious of ways. An actor in a present-day Broadway play, hiring a press agent to make capital of his appearance in the run, will find that the agent's fee is his entire week's salary. But in 1964, it cost a mere $40 a week to hire such a liaison with the press (you'd no guarantee, of course, that you'd make the papers that week, and had to pay up whether or not). When Andy and I would open his studio, even then always referred to as the "Factory," in the morning—if, say, we'd had a business breakfast with some gallery owner, financial advisor, or touring speculator—the first thing he'd do was drop a dime in the pay phone by the elevator in that floor-through loft on East Forty-Seventh and tell his press agent everywhere he'd gone and everything he'd done the night before, no matter how trivial or dull. This, like so much of his work, was a stroke of disarming but principled simplicity. Transparent, easy, even idiotic, after we've heard it. Except that he thought of it, and we didn't. And ultimately, enviably effective, for as an early-on, confessed seeker of celebrityship above all (even money), his fame would shortly rival that of Dali, Matisse, Pollock, and Picasso, no amateurs at courting international reputations themselves.

I also wish to note before going further that, though I'll be recording the specific things he said to me in relation to creating each film in so far as I recall them, generally speaking he really gave me very few instructions. His normal way of communicating was by staring at me and mumbling. That is to say that whatever he wanted and how I was to go about doing it was present in his concentration. Should I not be capable of reading that way, it was clear from the first that I would not be of much use to him. Discerning him was aggravated by his wearing nearly opaque, tinted glasses night and day, indoors and out, to protect the sensitivity of his iris, a conformity of his quasi-albino pigmentation. So it was very difficult to interpret his eyes in which, with most people, one would have those convenient "windows to the soul." In addition, he was quite the strangest looking person I've known closely: so besides my problem with standing up to authority, I did not care to too directly search his lips, jaws, or spider-broken skin while he was talking to me. I would avert my gaze when we were planning a film, registering him from the corner of my vision, sensitive to his shifting expression as the cat was to the camera lights, and depended a great deal on his tone or hesitations or retractions in wording, for he was laconic when he was pertinent, to understate the case. This sidelong dovetailing explains a lot about the indirectly angled products of the collaboration (e.g., *The Life of Juanita Castro, Kahuna!, Their Town, Hanoi Hanna*), and its uneasy industry (*Horse, Space*), and much about the lateral collaboration itself; and my way of coming to terms with him in its subsequent years, or why perhaps I hadn't any, for no death has had for me so disorienting an aftermath. Like the queen bees at the coffeehouse, there was no defecting from him with impunity. Real defection, in fact, would always be imaginary.

Fifty Fantasticks

Andy rented the large New Yorker Theatre on upper Broadway for an hour and a half early on the morning of December 20th 1964 for a private screening of *Harlot*. That way we could see what we had, or if we had anything, to spring on the public. On that house's state-of-the-art equipment, the film looked fine and the soundtrack was perfectly audible. — Too audible, for my taste.

I squinted in the bright sunlight of the world's most famous artery when we emerged from the pitch-black cinema, a blinking few seconds in which people always feel, and perhaps are, vulnerable. Waiting for that moment, Andy turned to me suddenly and said, "Come back to the Factory now, I want to take a roll of you."

"But I—I'm not prepared—I look like hell!" I stammered.

"No, it's O.K.," he returned, "you look great."

The Warhol Living Portraits got off the ground almost as soon as Andy started filming. They were done on three-minute silent reels. The subject was seated between the camera which squatted on a tripod and a blank, open projection screen. Andy would click on the camera and walk off. The portraits always were telling, in their way as much as or more so than ones on canvas. Mine was slated for inclusion in a feature called *Fifty Fantasticks*: as the title implies, a collection of fifty of these breathing portraits.

Gerard made double-frame stills from a number of these rolls, with the preceding frame above the slightly cropped

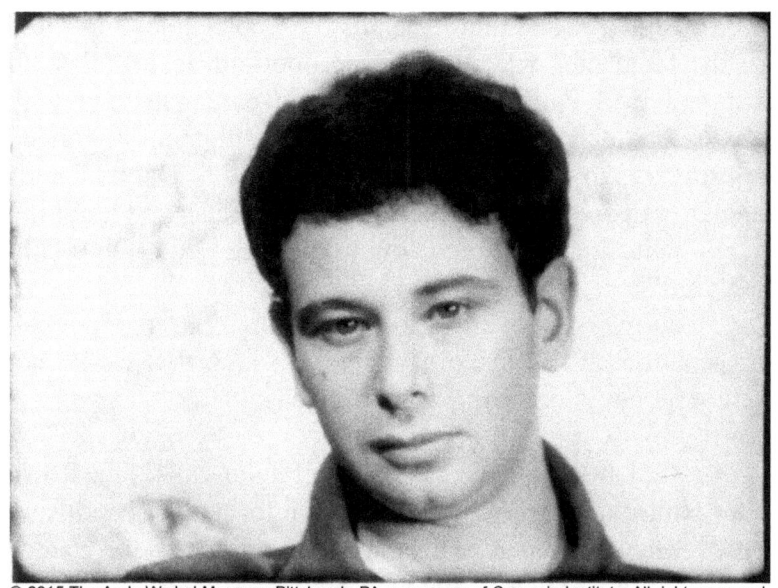

Ronald Tavel in Andy Warhol: "Fifty Fantasticks" (1964).

second, wrote a lyric to go with each, and published them in a huge and heavy softback called *Screen Tests*. As a result, film historians today call the 500 living portraits screen tests. They should not: they were far more final than that.

People always ask what it was like to sit for one of these. In a word, as you can imagine, uncomfortable. But since I had watched a number of other subjects go through the ordeal, I had a plan. Subjects advised each other it was best to have a plan. Otherwise the camera would "take over and get you." The extent to which the relentlessly grinding little eye was identified as an adversary is evident in actress Mary Woronov's portrait (1966). She relates to it with the uneasy hostility one normally reserves for an enemy in whose ugly corner sits all the advantage.

I decided to see that Bolex as the implacable Out-There in the form of a succulent hottie one had nevertheless to vamp. I lit a Pall Mall, relaxed, and came on to it with an understated twinkle, which understatement I gauged appropriate to a close shot. Factory pundits Danny Fields and Don Lyons, viewing the smoke-filled rush and laughing at its haute insolence and low humor, agreed: "Oh, yeah! It's you!"

Healthy, with even a touch of baby fat, the portrait presents me at my Factory happiest, a look that would not last long, but is flattering to say the least.

Drafted now into what Camille Paglia calls The Royal House of Warhol, it was protocol for me to accompany Andy when he appeared in public: occasionally for brunch at Serendipity's, then in the East Sixties — where we shortly discovered a blond, teenaged waiter, René Ricard, later a well-known poet and art critic — "Oh, how cute!" Andy enthused — but more often, in the evenings, at exclusive parties. Nights at the jammed, place-to-hold-court back room of Max's Kansas City on Park Avenue South and evenings at shindigs all over Manhattan are among my most persistent impressions of that era.

Most of all, there was the great and famous open house that Andy himself threw at the Factory. The crowded affair boasted attendance by Judy Garland, Zachary Scott, Freddie and Isabelle Eberstadt, and Montgomery Clift, whom I told I thought was "seasoned enough and ready now" to appear in a Warhol Flick (out of it, he said, blankly, "Thank you"); and stunning Rudy Nureyev, at the peak of his popularity, who danced feverishly with his male lover. Then he shattered the equipment of the paparazzo who snapped them in the act. I spoke to most everyone at that gala, for in the flushed expression of all present you could read their belief that they partied that moment not only in the center of New York's art life, but the world. Still, as a writer, I devoted the lion's share of my time to observing from the sidelines, and spent a lot of it in the company of the willowy, wide-eyed Mrs. Eberstadt, the daughter of Ogden Nash and patron of Jack Smith, a partner of mine in modeling at several of Smith's lengthy and legendary still-photography sessions. She was leaning against a major support post and couldn't move very far, having been "sewn" into her gorgeous gown for the evening, carried to the gala, then propped up against the pillar, and left there. "One must suffer for fashion," she instructed me gently, and I flashed that it was probably by just such public imprisonment that the lame Lord Byron had made his early rep in the Waltz Balls of 1812.

Yet despite the hectic hobnobs, whose frequency grew to six or seven a week, my strongest image of Andy in 1964 is the one he settled for on Christmas Eve, because I spent that night alone with him at the Factory. He worked through the long hours, crouching over sets of his Marilyn and Jackie silkscreens, spraying each with different primary colors and commenting to me the while on his choices. Then he moved some large Elvis Presley black and white double-images to a better stacking spot elsewhere in the studio, washed up, and dried his hands. It was past midnight; he would be spending what remained of the hours till dawn with his aged mother, and taking her to services in the morning.

It was quiet while he worked. I remember listening to the sound of the light, spaced traffic on Forty-Seventh Street. He spoke straight, he made no jokes, he asked my opinion of the finished silkscreens and some people coming and going in the loft at the time. He told me that alone amongst them, he found me always calm and oddly self-possessed. He inquired, expecting no answer, as to why that was.

He cabbed me to where I wanted to be, then instructed the driver to go on up Third and take him home.

Screen Test

In those days—late 1964, early 1965—Andy Warhol's lover was Philip Norman Fagan. Surprisingly little is known about him. He is remembered now largely for his appearance in *Harlot*, his performance in *Screen Test*, and the ambitious film project Andy planned around him, a work here and there obliquely referred to as *Aging*.

So little, in fact, is recoverable about this young man that he commonly is alluded to more in discussion of my work at the Factory than in any mention of his murky relationship with Andy—for it was Philip who prevailed upon the artist to make me a scenarist, and Philip who made sure that that happened.

In the cynical language of the day, Philip, out of earshot, would have been called a "twinkie." That is, a presentable young man, literally presentable everywhere he might have to be presented, relatively cultivated or good at faking as much, who always and above all was enviable for his looks. In short, the perfect roommate and escort, one who made his companion feel important at home and superior in public— to wit: would anyone else in any plausible place be likely to be so eye-catchingly accompanied?

A toy-boy, then, of the relatively well-heeled, relatively arrived gay. But while Hollywood had its established twinkie call-in agencies, of the free-lancers in this service on the East Coast, often more was expected—and delivered. For a number of such charmers set their sights on the most talented and renowned in homosexual circles, and further flattered themselves by fancying that, in line with their qualifications, they had suitably singled out their target for his genius and accomplishment rather than renown.

Self-deluding Philip was among these. Albeit highly selectively, he'd attached himself in the course of time to more than a few comfortably situated, somewhat older gay intellectuals. But he found an uncommon, not to say insurmountable, challenge in Andy, for Andy appeared to expect from Philip everything that his appeal and profession suggested. Not just the lip service and the illusion, but the goods.

To Andy's displeasure, these in time were not forthcoming.

For starters, Mr. Fagan did not put out. To be sure, it is rife in this pretending-not-to-be-a-paid-companion racket to hold that once you've gone to Promethean extent with the mark's sexual fantasies about you, you've nowhere else to take the affair and, in effect, unwittingly stamped it yourself with its expiry date. But Philip actually had problems in this area. As the *Screen Test* script implies, he related to the nates and male seam in distancing fetishes, and the contemplating of, let alone submission to sex induced near panic. Andy had said, and on occasion seemed to believe, that imagined sex was more fulfilling than physical love—an obvious rationalization that sympathizers at the time had the taste not to challenge. Still, this configuration enabled the affair to go a few rounds, indeed, to be at all.

Philip could bake a mean cake, though, and deflected Andy's advances by teaching him to as well, and letting Julia Warhola, Andy's widowed mother, judge the results. A down-to-basics kind of guy myself, I found all this to be girlish and silly, but it was relatively harmless and fit neatly into Andy's well-documented food and food-preparation devotionals.

Ultimately, and sad to say, it was not Philip's ambition

that did him in, but that he hadn't the gray matter to ground its eagle precinct. Let's say men didn't trip over each other to get his attention because they wanted to discuss Hegel and Hume.

The artist had met the engaging Black Irish seafarer at a concert in 1964. To Philip's persuasive credit, he became the first love-interest Andy ever invited to reside in his townhouse at 1342 Lexington Avenue, in whose basement Julia lived. It was Andy's eye for the slightest alteration, holding Philip's then unusually continuous image, that gave Andy the idea for *Aging*, literally, a time-exposure project. As the story went, it was to be three-minute, stationary-Bolex close-shots of Philip taken daily and spanning six months, hopefully six years. It was to document a truly traditional, not to say romantic, subject: that of finding ourselves here, "Where youth grows pale, and spectre-thin, and dies... where Beauty cannot keep her lustrous eyes/ or new Love pine at them tomorrow."

This accounts for the 103 hitherto unaccounted for three-minute takes that we have of Philip Fagan and the lack of clear labeling intent on their rolls, which has confused researchers. They are unlabeled because Andy was silently furious at having to abandon this above-the-reach-of-criticism film entry in his series of eschatological studies. Paradoxically, the "reality-recording" filmmaker-painter thought nothing of painting over history.

We owe that abandonment to the fact that Philip was possessive, as only the asexual can be, and determined to rid his playing field of any and all competition—an obvious impossibility since a factory and its workers were so central to the whole Warholian concept and modus operandi. His primary target was Gerard, however hard to understand why, but ultimately he wanted the Factory emptied of everybody except myself. Not only did he appear to conceive of me as no rival, but as an actual aid and potential benefactor. He proposed to Andy that I, on the proof of my fiction, should be put to creating screenplays for him, which Andy would direct. He also thought these scripts should feature no one but himself and, that being the case, the Factory should be downsized—with all they assembly-lined there forthwith pink-slipped. The remarkable thing is the degree to which the smittened entertained this strategy.

Thus, in the course of a long Merce Cunningham-style Dead Chicken Dance Concert staged shortly thereafter at the Judson Memorial Church, Andy instructed me to come up with a seventy-minute scenario for Philip. The noisy, hip audience was reclined on the sprawling floor of the cavernous nave and the dance troupe occasionally came through this unruly roost throwing real and/or rubber chicken corpses at it. Andy spotted silver-screen promise in the good-time crowd, and felt that the informality of the proceedings would support our diluted concentration while zigzagging our way amongst it, soliciting here and there future film talent. He was teaching me never to let pleasure totally replace business. During this art-filled, or art-flung, walk he in effect proposed our collaboration, the brain-child of, and present to, a hard-to-please lover.

S *creen Test* was the most intimately filmed of our combined efforts, and is the most intimate portrait we have of any of Warhol's lovers. It introduces my off-camera character called Tester's Voice, a disembodied examiner intent on humiliating the auditioner; and whose exasperation and vehemence grow when the intended victim becomes unimaginative in response, reticent, evasive, or withdrawn.

In the first reel, Philip is reminded of an unpleasant incident that puzzled him, his shoplifting of a pair of red panties he'd convinced himself he intended as a gift to a girl. The memory is interlaced with painful misgivings concerning his father, then brother, for his convoluted relations with them actually caused the shoplifting. He evidently conjures up for himself on screen a forceful and incestuous image of the insteps of both these men. Then he quietly struggles as he relives his guilty transference of them to the girl—which guilt has sought asssuagement in his being caught shoplifting. This disturbing, foot dual-substituent reflects interestingly on Warhol's own full-blown foot fetish (besides linking the lovers in a way that needs no comment); and the foot theme with sadistic (i.e., punishing) imagery is reprised a few months later in Tosh Carrillo's performance as Max in *Horse*. The theme and images of guilt assuagement (via policewoman sadism and legal retaliation) through shoe shoplifting and transference to a girl is reprised, of course, in the even better known film shot the following year, *Hedy, or the Fourteen-Year-Old Girl*.

Screen Test enters a second phase when the Tester seems to be entertaining an infatuation with Philip's close-up itself, his head tilted slightly to the left, and he lulls that image with a sonnet. But Philip, who would have heard hidden references to Gerard in the sonnet ("he can write beautiful poems"), grows suspicious, distrustful, and taciturn. He watches me warily through the corner of his light-reflecting eye for much of the insight-dwindling denouement.

I had found this making of Philip's portrait very tense, both because of the patience needed to knead Philip, and Andy's anxiety and bewilderment while enduring the actor's pervasive equivocality. This following his insistence on his performance resourcefulness. I live with an everlasting afterimage of Andy hovering over the Auricon directly to my right. Time has weighted it with the burden of what I now know he required this film to be and the decision which he, as I was to learn, was reaching rapidly.

I was also disoriented by the ordeal of being caught between the two of them. Because it should have been suffocating. And wasn't.

One afternoon a few weeks later I found Andy spraying white, pink, and red primaries on the petals of the poppy flower silkscreens. The paintings were laid on the floor in flush squares in the sunlight from Forty-Seventh, and he squatted, literally, on top of them while he selected a color can, sprayed one flower at a time, and reflected on the result. He looked up at me long enough to say, "Philip likes you. But he doesn't like anyone else. I don't think he understands what we're doing here. I asked him not to come back."

Edited and assumptive, as would be most of his pronouncements to me, it held the compliment and dubious observation that I, as well as the other studio denizens, did understand what he was up to (and, of course, a warning). I believe this delusion testifies to a certain common self-induced naivety, perhaps for his own survival, which I'd like to underline. For as the confessions of the surviving Factory workers show, in memoirs, interviews, sound bites, and panel chats, few there were who took the trouble to think about what he was doing back then, or in all the intervening years.

In a display of perceived betrayal and habitual retaliation, Andy refused to release *Screen Test*. After his sudden departure, Philip tried his luck in other gay milieux, beginning with the cream of the Beat experimenters. William Burroughs's close associate and collaborator, Brion Gysin, found him uncommonly attractive and invited Philip to go through his sales pitch in and around the Chelsea Hotel. But Gysin remembered me as having referred to Philip once as "a bad boy." He told me the statement had perplexed him at first, but that afterward, having grown wise to the young man's unbending chastity, he knew what I meant. So Philip felt that for the time being, he'd played New York for about what it was worth.

As if he were in need of any addition to his romantic appeal, Philip, being actually a tattooed sailor and erstwhile merchant marine, was on speaking terms with wide stretches of Central America and the Far East, notably Hong Kong. Declining in fortune and reverting to type, as it were, Philip discovered himself later that year on a yacht in the South Pacific. There, apparently, his virginity cut less ice and was, we speculated, in the confines of the cabin multiply displaced. He managed to send a Christmas card and later an S.O.S. to Andy, claiming to be a prisoner on this yacht and pleading to be rescued, but Andy, in the first of a roll call of such reactions in front of me, said, "Good for him!"

Not long after, Philip Norman Fagan, professional trophy boy, died in the South China Sea. His large tattoo, which had so riveted my fancy and distracted me during the filming of *Screen Test*, was a seventeenth-century scythe-bearing and cloaked skeleton, memento mori of Death on Wings.

Screen Test #2

At the time of this writing (summer 2001), *Screen Test #2* is the most rented movie in the Museum of Modern Art's Circulating Film Library. *Screen Test #2* no doubt owes its popularity to theorist Douglas Crimp's influential essay "Mario Montez: For Shame"[2] and the favorable word of mouth from those who decided to investigate Dr. Crimp's observations. Yet this entry has always been painful for me to watch, and I avoided doing so even after its restoration and until May 13, 2001, when, at a screening at the Podewil Institute in Berlin during the Rich and Famous Arts Festival, I was forced to study it, knowing I would shortly be subjected to a rigorous Q & A. To my great relief, it was enthusiastically received; and a week later proved of equal interest at a seminar in Zurich.

The film, essentially a relentless inquisition, poses some difficult questions. Am I, in my heard but unseen role, delivering a carefully studied performance as a neurotic and sadistic administer of screen tests, or are we being confronted with a gay man's real-life projecting of his self-hatred onto a blatantly defenseless transvestite? Is it possible that the transvestite, Mario Montez, doesn't know that the occasion is simply a Warhol movie and not a genuine screen test—for Hugo's *Notre Dame de Paris* no less, a melodrama which Warhol would be incapable of realizing even if he had wanted to and he most certainly would not have? In addition,

---

2 In Douglas Crimp, *"Our Kind of Movie": the Films of Andy Warhol,* Cambridge: MIT Press, 2012.

since I wrote and, to all visible and audible evidence, am also directing and starring in this effort, why is it called an Andy Warhol film? This last question, raised by grim-faced student viewers in Berlin and Zurich, was again posed in relation to *The Life of Juanita Castro* on June 1st at the huge and sprawling, U.S. State Department-sponsored Andy Warhol Festival in Moscow.

We shall never have a satisfactory answer to the first problem. All interviews, no matter how perfunctory, all public statements and appearances involve a performance. To a certain extent, so does any situation in which we are remotely uncomfortable but manage to hold our own. This is one of the meanings of *Screen Test #2*. And bear in mind the pressure I was under to extract something dramatic from Mario's presence in the proscribed seventy minutes, no editing permitted. As for Mario, his contribution centers on the ease, the speed with which he accepts that this, his dream—auditioning for and then possibly being featured in a major celluloid epic—is real. Asked in Berlin if Mario ever spoke to me again after the shoot, I said, "Of course he did. Every American wants to be in movies." *Screen Test #2* was, to be sure, an ordeal for him: but many have given their lives for less than what he achieved—the central attention in a work that will outlast most of Hollywood's.

As for the third quandary, Andrew Sarris, reviewing *Juanita*, perhaps gave the straightest response: "that Warhol has assumed the role of mere metteur-en-scène" while I, by implication, assumed that of régie. Our collaboration would remain more or less that way until the interference sometime in July of 1965.

Callie Angell claimed that *Screen Test* and *Screen Test #2*, if shown together, would be sufficient for a course on gender studies. Because in the first, Philip resists the insinuations of my goading and eventually retreats into the sustained-by-silence, accepted "macho" pretense of the day; while in the second, Mario falls for the bait, hook, line, and gender-bending sinker. As a result, the latter effort flows neatly and looks carefully constructed. It corners the viewer's interest almost at once with the unbelievably extended and cooperatively created "diarrhea" sequence, then drops back to a quiet note and from there slowly builds to an appalling climax.

The images of Underground transvestite star Mario Montez have not only withstood the test of time, he has more fans now than ever—a tribute, no doubt, to his charm, focus, and sly wit, because he could not act his way out of a paper bag.

René Rivera was a jauntily stepped New Yorican, unassuming in appearance, in deportment almost self-effacing. He was gentle, soft-spoken, and vulnerable. He had large, attractive eyes and a small, quick-to-smile mouth with a lot of character at its corners. The filmmaker, art theorist, and architect Jack Smith must be credited with having "molded" him. He trained René first as a model for his early still photography and, promising him fame and fortune, claimed the boy never took a bad picture. His concentration was complete, and a legible, specific idea arranges his features in every print that survives today. Baptizing him with the unfortunate screen name Dolores Flores, Smith cast him as the Spanish Dancer in his still-litigious 1963 masterpiece, *Flaming Creatures*. He later talked René into the weighty signatory of Mario Montez, in honor of Hollywood's "Undisputed Queen of Technicolor," Maria Montez, in whose silver lamé gowns and platformwedgies René felt he not only fit, but strode with hereditary regality. Sadly, he neither looked like nor gave the faintest fidelity to an impression of the late West Indian femme fatale. However, what he could approximate was her belief—belief when he was in a scene that it was not a movie-shoot at all, but the real thing.

When Mario tired of Smith's sporadic use of him (he'd complain: "Jack's keeping me under wraps—and I told him I only have five years of beauty left!"), he restlessly looked about for other venues. And Andy, who stayed in touch with most events in the Underground, was quickly alerted.

Although, as mentioned above, "screen tests" is an inaccurate label for Andy's stationary-Bolex, three-minute, one-person film studies, he nevertheless was intrigued with the notion of the screen test. This because of its error-free simplicity, its indisputable portraiture, and its deconstructive sense of pre-a-particular-film—even "pre" the medium of film, as would follow from his trajectory to recapitulate the medium's history. Fascinated with its possibilities, Warhol wanted another go at a feature using the same format as Philip Fagan's *Screen Test*. "Mario will be better, he'll react more," he advised me. So giving some thought to the aims of this specialist in silkscreen stenciling, who studiously avoided and studiously assaulted the stenciling of any nation's cinema language in his own turn to cinema, I whipped up notes for a *Screen Test #2* and, fifteen days after Philip's trial, administered Mario's.

But the atmosphere (as integral to the method) created for the making of this film differed radically from its predecessor. Replacing the privacy I'd counted on as de rigueur to such an intimate examination was now the Factory's ever-opening elevator doors: and that established a protocol for nearly all the shoots to come—which were to gather a momentum climaxing in something akin to carnival events.

Mario arrived early on the afternoon of February 7th, and spent hours at the back of the Factory getting into costume. It would not be accurate to claim he ever got into character: the costume was his character. All the more surprising because of the time he wastes during this head-shot two-reeler in worrying-to-a-rag, around his frightful auburn wig, a dark bandanna that looks like a hapless rag to begin with.

In this try my character, called Tester's Voice, is out for blood. In fact, the "voice of the serpent," evidently antagonized by Mario's bland, matter-of-course responses, approaches dementia, an exhibition as unbridled as it is obscene. Mario appears to listen with purpose to my instructions and, sometimes hemming and hawing but never surrendering to the fury almost anyone else would have entertained here, to carry through on all of them. What makes this movie so suspenseful is that Mario, besides believing that this is real, accepts it as a perfectly normal screen test—which, pathetic and distressing, he hasn't the talent to take. The viewer—and myself!—as I say, remain forever frustrated by his declining the many opportunities I gave him to quite justifiably rise to an on-screen outrage.

His performance, in part, is as an audience to my off-screen emoting: a common phenomenon in Warhol cinema. That is, we infer what is happening out-of-frame by reading the in-frame reaction to it. Andy later told an interviewer that he didn't understand the psychology of my off-camera behavior. A bit nonplused by this movie's autonomy, we both subsequently kept up the pretense that the personality being studied here is Mario.

René Rivera, as good as his word, did indeed bow out at the end of his stipulated five years and moved to north Florida. Once there, he refused to acknowledge a star named

Mario Montez and in time married, settled down, and raised children.

Some notes: The Geek section can be traced to my having caught *Nightmare Alley* on TV that month. Tyrone Power's favorite role, it is a noir classic which fascinated me as a child. The time allotted to *Notre Dame de Paris* is because I'd wanted to do something dramatic with it since early adolescence. Plus, Mario obviously summons up La Esmeralda, a benevolent but dopey gypsy dancer. Later, in the summer, when Andy asked me what I myself would like to film and I proposed adapting the Hugo novel, he said it wasn't the kind of thing he thought he should do: a period piece, a narrative, a costume melodrama, etc. He thus confessed how unrelated he is to the late sixties and early seventies Morrissey melodramas he merely would produce.

The "diarrhea" sequence, eerily recalling what Michael Moon has suggested in dissecting Andy's half-dozen cartoon-lifted paintings, probably owes more to the word's disconcerting sound and spelling, its luna and mother-goddess components, and its melding of diamonds with a giant bird. The line about strangling a pet panther named Patricia is original—we had a lot of fun thoroughly exhausting it in the heavily improvised stage versions of *Screen Test*. The idea germinated while I was watching a banquet scene in DeMille's *Sign of the Cross*, in which a drunk Sybarite, upbraiding a demented courtesan with a leopard in tow, says something to the effect of: "Thy kisses are for beasts, my beauty—but not for me!"

Screen Test #2 was released to a generally favorable, even condescendingly sentimental reception; its stills, at least, have been extensively, if patronizingly, inspected over three decades. Its persistent image of Mario batting his false eyelashes for posterity is frequently reproduced. I stuck close to the text throughout the bout, a model of bad taste which upset pseudo-liberals in the sixties and, I take pride in reporting, will irritate the politically correct and unsophisticated in its spanking off-focused, 1996-restored print.

Suicide

In my novel *Street of Stairs* I had used a Mediterranese
or North African esperanto and broken English for poetic
effect, double-entendres, and the inadvertent meaning in
moments. So it was natural that when Andy ordered the third
scripted film to premiere at a Factory party to be thrown
a brief twenty-seven days after Mario's "orals" had been
lensed—and told me to fashion it around a young European
who spoke in seductive and arresting broken English—that
expeditiously I would, listening to him, "hear" *Suicide* well
in advance of writing it, as a long poem.

As the lending of a podium in the form of a poem to
a generalized outcry of international youth in the mid-
sixties, it stands by itself among Andy's movies, and is the
biggest surprise in the post-mortem disclosure of suppressed
filmwork.

But it does not stand alone among the artist's concerns
or subject matter. In fact, it has a vivid position in one of
his most dynamic groupings, the disaster series. And so for
those analysts for whom Andy's move to film was not only
necessary but his aesthetically most important, *Suicide* is
certain to galvanize a deal of attention in the future.

Rock B. was a *Gentleman's Quarterly*-chic and trim,
classically small-featured French film actor who jet-set his
time in a kind of frenzy between expensive hotels on either
side of the Atlantic. In that shuffle, he was symptomatic
of a considerable block of the weekly Factory drop-ins,
and contributed strongly to my overall impression then of
the traffic through the artworld landmark. But it was in

his guise of a multiply wrist-slashing, would-be suicide that he interested Andy, and I thought should be rendered representative.

Taking a pencil and pad, I went to interrogate him in what I had to make my standard pre-script practice with strangers. This visit always frightened the interviewees, but as we've come to accept from daytime TV talk shows, one has only to ask and the secret-keepers will tell all, Rock and his compelling double life included. To be sure, this reaction would be grist for the mill of a future berative essay in the form of a feature, *Vinyl*. But then, since I never saw myself as an intimidating person, I felt the fear and confessions I elicited from prospective performers were a result of my bodying-in for the "Ghostlike Power," particularly as, and whenever, he was disliked, a notion reconfirmed for me as recently as the November 1994 Warhol Weekend Film Festival in L.A. There, scattered survivors of his sixties activities showed up to get even with his Ghost by assailing me, in the belief they'd cherished in the belief-aggravating interval that I, who might have rescued them in those long-done days, had stood writer-voyeuristically by instead to witness the Andyan tender mercies of their victimization and spiritual demolition. Back when it was all happening, none surrendered his better judgment to such an interpretation of Pop Art's fallout with more gusto than Rock, who seemed altogether uncertain that Andy was a fully-paid-up member of the human race.

The script or blueprint of *Suicide* also is unusual in being so extensively self-explaining, not just of its distinct filming process but of what actually did transpire that evening in the crowded, press- and idler-filled Factory.

In frame of the stationary camera was to be Rock's belly-up wrists, side by side between his seated knees. I would hold the script he'd not seen before that night up at a comfortable distance from his eyes and safely out of camera range. On it, he is clearly instructed to read all his own lines while I read (and play) everyone else in his life needed to let breathe the circumstances that led to each attempt at suicide. But Rock has both written above words to translate or clarify the English for himself (edifying further, with a compendium of his English) and crossed out others and provided substitutes, this latter largely to conceal his homosexuality and on occasion the identity of certain celebrities peripherally involved in his misfortunes. How crucial some felt it was to cover their minority sexuality in those days could not be more graphic than the living record this movie makes of that.

Andy took a copy of the *Suicide* script as soon as I finished it, which was just before the shoot, and scanned it. (All the original scenarios were warehoused with his acquisitions, though some were unconscionably offered at the posthumous auctions.) Then, shortly before the camera rolled, he ordered a voluptuous, varied bouquet of festively colored, huge flowers from a local florist. "Since this is in Technicolor," was all he said to me with a sidewise turn of his head that always signaled he knew I understood and was in accord. But aside from thuswise incorporating this film into his extensive four-flower poppy painting series, at that point at the height of its creative fervor and evidently the most attention-getting project he'd embarked on up until then, its ulterior motive was probably to surprise me, as the writer and director of *Suicide*, as my script was intended to surprise Rock and record the result. For unless it is conceded that the writer and director are as much a part of what is being filmed as the (other) players, the full scope of Warhol's perceptive intentions and, perhaps, achievement will not be understood. In this sense—that the record we have, i.e., the actual film, differs from the scenario or is a selection of its thrusts and proposals—the scripts exist in a kind of dialogue with the films, and side by side with them.

So I picked, per vignette of suicide-try, a sunflower, tuberose, or Bird of Paradise from the bouquet for Rock to grind between his shaking fingers—thus replacing the script's call for (symbolic) spoons, razor, a tomato and diary. A basin was set under his hands against the young man's shoes, and I then was to pour water from a pitcher over his scarlet scars and into the basin each time we reached the actual attempt in the self-destructive roll call. (Of course, the water pouring stood in for the boy's blood pour, but this is irremediable in Warhol's thinking, his maddening simplicity, idiotic and irrefutable.)

Disorienting Rock more than me was the swaying assembly of what appeared to him to be morbidly curious gossip-mongers and yellow-rag photographers: for by now I was inured to them and, besides, had a lot of work, acting and thinking, to do here as the script makes plain. But they amounted to an unexpected, public confessional for him, which added to the agony of our reliving his life's most unhappy—and self-absorbed—moments.

At last, he reached down to the nearly full basin, lifted it up, and poured its contents completely over me. As Rock started for the elevator, Andy broke from the crowd wringing his hands and rushed to my side. Then he searched my face and, as I was totally soaked, asked with the concern of an alarmed mother, "Oh, Ronnie, should we stop?"

Observers think this (show of) distress is unique in the relentless neo-verité the artist practiced, but when I insisted that we continue until the second reel ended, it wasn't to remind him that he was trying to sidestep the classical rigor to which, and by which, he held me. It was simply that I couldn't break the momentum of the experience for myself, what I was first understanding enacting Rock's terrors, and that I had to finish it out then for better or worse, having the presence of mind right there to know no attempt would or could be made to re-do the staging of these peculiarly surface traumas.

I probably had not been so involved before in the "fiction" of a filming—that is, living the recreation as if it were all initially now—for I'd felt neither the drenched discomfort nor the humiliation of those moments, though I'd a vague sense of the somber-level leveling occurring there in my humorous martyrdom for art. Instead, I was driven to see, gratuitously, that this excruciation be articulated: and for that reason later would hold myself responsible, along with *Vinyl*'s screen- and stage-version actors, for the mutual-consent torture which creates that work's principal speculation.

That evening's film ends with a sad, long look at the broken flowers in the re-set basin while I, now playing Rock as well as his familiars, drone the misadventures on to a conclusion.

The aftermath: It still being winter, I came down with a good cold; Rock returned when the Factory was nearly deserted and stole a painting for his pains. Warhol did not accommodate art thefts and considered it ample remuneration for the spoiled ingrate.

Film history has forgotten that European's other contributions, but this portrait of bewildered, groundless aristocracy in his World War II-hungover generation remains vivid in its zeitgeist plea, as unforgiving as it is unforgivable.

The Life of Juanita Castro

In February of 1965 I was writing poems, essays, promotionals, and dozens of letters as well as the screenplays. But I did not feel as pressured as I often have doing a lot less. I felt receptive. What appeared to be an innocent enough invitation to dinner became thus one of the most important evenings in my life.

Fidel Castro's brother-in-law, Waldo Dias-Balart, was living in exile in the center of the row of beautiful nineteenth-century townhouses on the north (Tenth Street) side of Tompkins Square Park. Tall, hirsute, and wealthy, he'd gotten off the island when the getting was good, with most of his fortune intact. I myself had visited Cuba after Castro was in office and before travel there for Americans was banned. I'd written short light verse and serious long poems about Cuba, knew a number of Cuban dancers-in-exile and nightclub entertainers and one celebrated stage and soap star, had several close Cuban friends and a Cuban lover, and had been introduced by Andy to two very charming, politically active Cuban sisters, Aniram Anipso and Mercedes Ospina. I indeed had stood in Havana and watched Fidel deliver one of his eight-hour speeches, in which, riveting my attention, he made extensive, theatrical use of a great white handkerchief. A Havanan standing beside me dryly observed that their President craved a similar handkerchief so he could have something to stick his nose into.

Some weeks before *Suicide* was lensed, Waldo invited Andy and the immediate protégés to dinner. We sat around a classically extended, elegant table in the splendid home.

Basking as I was in the full light of his favor that week, Andy made certain I was the cynosure of the entourage: in a seat from which I at least felt myself to be at a perfect vantage. A few drinks and naturally enough the conversation turned to the Cuban revolution and its political intrigues, particularly the in-fighting on the part of the Castro siblings, and most particularly the prima-donna deprecation of the vociferous and flamboyant older sister, Juanita. Andy became fascinated and said we should do the life story of Juanita Castro—that he had the issue of *Life* magazine (compulsory reading for him) in which this anti-communist critic of the Prime Minister roundly denounced him. ("My Brother Is a Tyrant and He Must Go," August 28, 1964, pp. 22-38)

But it was the tone of what Waldo said that night, his peculiar indifference, distance, amusement, and sang-froid concerning his homeland and the missile crisis of October 25-28, 1962, that nearly brought this world to an end, that made a permanent impression on me. Unfortunately, I cannot recall a single sentence, thought, bon mot, description, or even idea of what he expressed—and being so mainmast situated among the island's movers and shakers, Waldo knew whereof he spoke. All of it amazed me in a deep, undramatic way as if, fixed on and mesmerized by Waldo's twisting of his black walrus mustachios, I were at the center of a vast whorl in that room, in all its Samuel Goldwyn sumptuousness, and all of it existed for me, and all of it, whirling about me with its orbit rapidly shrinking, came to center in my chest.

What I beheld/intuited/understood is what I think of as the political vision, which, however abbreviated, elaborated, or attenuated, never would alter essentially throughout all the matter I'd subsequently mine for political themes. To date, that material makes up twenty to twenty-five percent of my drama production. And that is why, although it so frequently is commented upon in statistics on trivia or even encyclopedias, it was no surprise to me that a script so pre-set and balanced in my mind would be written, on February 20, 1965, in just three hours. Or become the most praised of the movies I wrote and directed, and in its theatrical recycling my most produced play.

Everything works for *The Life of Juanita Castro*. Including the unforeseen, the mistakes, the last-minute or fortuitous changes. Its purpose is to be a film and to be a film without error, and it is that, no more, no less. It generates idea after idea, literally ceaselessly. It argues that nothing other than itself is a movie and it forecloses refutation. It is exclusive.

As all things come together in this piece, the medium and its matter, so the collaboration comes together—meaning Warhol's energy and purpose and the whole machinery of the Factory setup which he places at my disposal. I think not I, nor anyone outside of himself, would ever again make such happy use of it.

I wrote the on-camera director role for Andy himself to play, but in a crucial decision, holding the script in his hand and showing no discernible calculation or feeling, he turned it over to me. I wrote the titular role for Mario Montez, but in what would be the underground's luckiest declination of duty ("Ronnie, I don't do politics or religion"), we were spared his coy mannerisms and blessed with Marie Menken, arriving for what she thought was to be simply a rehearsal of her role as Raul: only to find herself instead starring in the movie's one and only take. The Warhol flash again: ignoring her gender ("Ronnie, what difference does it make?"), he offered Marie a few beers in exchange for her performance. "I'm not an actress," she insisted. "But you are an audience," I responded.

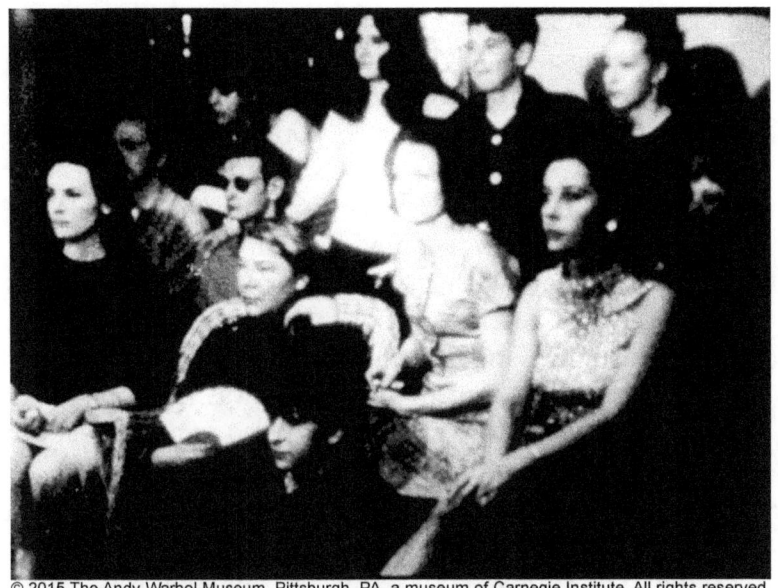

Ronald Tavel (top row center) as the Director, Elektrah Lobel on his right as Raul Castro. Second row (from left): Waldo Dias-Balart, Harvey Tavel (with dark glasses), Mercedes Ospina as Fidel, Isabelle Collin Dufresne (later known as Ultra Violet). Front row: Aniram Anipso as Che Guevara, Marie Menken (with fan) as Juanita in Andy Warhol: "The Life of Juanita Castro" (1965).

"What does that mean?"

"Sit down. We'll show you."

This work is not so much an example of making the most of one's limitations as making an asset of one's liabilities. At the time, people thought Andy silk-screened because he couldn't sketch or paint. While we know now that nothing could be further from the truth, this film appeared to be part of that strategy. But actually it wasn't. I read their lines and screen directions to the performers not because they would not have learned these themselves or rehearsed—during the first half of that year, the chances are they would have—but because there was no more intention to have the participants "act" as acting normally is understood than there was to move the camera. And because Andy wanted to teach me a lesson. And, indirectly, the whole world of filmmakers, film watchers.

There will always be the question of whether or not he grasped what had been accomplished with this film. I expect that the art theorists and historians who mold the way Andy is interpreted will answer that according to whatever the current fashion is in perceiving him. It is wrong to believe that every successful aesthetic maneuver or result was intentional and wholly conscious on his part, but it is also wrong to believe for a moment that that is what he was working for.

Clearly, it was more a matter of searching for a process that would make talk, would make accountable, everything sucked into its vortex; a process whose ambition was, as has been art's since men became conscious of it, a search for truth. That is why it was so irksome and puzzling to have commentators at the time claim that Andy was anti-art, and to have subsequent producers of my plays request that I delete from promotional material references to my "stint" at the Factory.

This filmscript was staged without any changes in its dialogue or mise en scène. The sense of watching people watching in their mind's eye was retained—in their visual imagination, as it were, for they are watching the director's performance, who always, crucially, is above and behind them. The major difference between stage and screen, of course, is that the film exploits the advantage of having a script that comes as a surprise to its participants. Single performances at, say, universities, can adopt this procedure easily enough, but no run of the play could afford a nightly change in cast. To be sure, at theatres where large and loose companies were available, there have been weekly changes of cast. Other times, casts developed stylistic approximations of surprise or unities whose resistance and resilience and/or highly circumscribed improvisations tended to compensate. But performances have been ruined by cutesy, extensive rebelliousness, embellishments, and baroque elaborations.

If good-natured, the piece is affably severe and needs to be kept that way. If political, the subject matter may be more the relation of politics to aesthetics than a particular political situation. The work's life and energy obviously derive from a festering family argument, but the family argument is anything but a mere if central metaphor. It is the frightening point.

Bitch

A ndy was so enthralled with Marie Menken's performance in *The Life of Juanita Castro* that the following Sunday he had Gerard Malanga and soundman-cameraman Buddy Wirtschafter pack up all the filming equipment and haul it off for an on-location shoot: the Brooklyn Heights penthouse apartment of Ms. Menken and her professor-husband, perky Willard Maas.

The hope, obviously, was that the charismatic matron Andrew Sarris was to describe as looking like a lady longshoreman would reprise her silver screen winning-way, a mixture of beady-eyed alcoholic bewilderment, fishwife shrewdness and shrewishness, sudden baby-like bellowing, and a sorrow with which almost anyone could identify.

But no such thing was to happen. Altogether too lauded, and too self-conscious now, Marie, for the purposes of performance, was forever ruined by her admirers. Faced with the relentlessly grinding Auricon, she found confabulatory improvisation without the cicerone of a scenario more than she could master. When the inevitable gallons of drink were brought forth by Willard to prompt her narrations or inspire her outbursts, she was lit in no time at all and, under the great pressure of having to be instantly great, actually passed out.

B uddy Wirtschafter, a filmmaker and filmmaking teacher at the School of Visual Arts, had been drafted for service on *Juanita Castro*, specifically, to tech it out to circumvent the soft focus blurring the handful of films preceding it. Recalled to duty on *Bitch*, he discovered setting up in the romantically antique but dollhouse-scaled rooftop suite no easy enterprise, and had particular trouble with the second reel sound. But Buddy would work at my side throughout the entire busy spring of 1965, and I came to think of him as a very upbeat, if slightly tipsy, right-hand man who made the most of equipment that was anything but state-of-the-art, in often less than optimal circumstances.

Back in January of the year, Andy had taken me to another penthouse, that of well-heeled Hollywood movie producer Lester Persky, when Lester was throwing a celebrity-thickened soirée there. (I got stuck in the stalled elevator with Tennessee Williams, who appeared to find every time-passing commentary I offered over his head.) Clasping a cocktail glass in one hand, and a cigarette holder in the other, and standing in the center of the party parlor when I finally entered was an arresting twenty-two-year-old blueblood sporting a brunette beehive, a leopard-skin evening outfit, and a pair of the largest brown eyes I was ever to have discombobulate me. "Nyoka, the Jungle Girl!" I exclaimed. "Do you think so?" she returned smiling irresistibly, and dare I say it, a fire deeply retreated in the iris a-dance at her dilated pupils? "Oh, yes!" I hastened to reinforce, "we'll have you over to the Factory and shoot the grainy, all-new adventures of Nyoka. No one's done her justice since Republic's backlot forties cliffhanger." And Miss Edith Minturn Sedgwick was very pleased.

We saw nor hide nor hair of her for a good month, and then she emanated from the elevator to beguile her afternoon watching the *Juanita Castro* shoot. Being a fruit fly from the word go, and so seizing upon Andy's circle as a comfortable and unthreatening salon she just might make her hangout, Edie reappeared for the lensing of *Bitch*. This time, however, when Marie Menken became intractable, she found herself incorporated into the proceedings—in a "don't just stand around, earn your keep" kind of way; but, green to any kind of enterprise involving real effort, Edie was able to add very little—except, of course, her lilting laughter.

Both Marie and Willard were underground filmmakers themselves, and visible in Manhattan's art and academic world. Willard had been Gerard's professor and mentor out at Staten Island College: it was he, in fact, who had introduced Gerard to Andy. Marie and Willard were each fifty-three at the time and, though Willard was aggressively bisexual, an admirable seducer to say the least, they had a grown child and were still very much in love: a love that is obvious and touching when Willard serves Marie her mood-alteratives in *Bitch*'s first reel.

I had come late to the location shoot, if memory serves, to deliver the manuscript of *The Banana Diary*. When I got up there, I walked into what I felt was the halting progress of a fairly hopeless over-effort. In the reel break, Marie warned Andy she wanted to pitch Campbell soups, that she'd grown up on them; but Andy, concerned that winter over possible litigation with Campbell's, told her not to. (The suit—for infringement of copyright, or art theft, as it were—ended amicably with the company's vice-president forking over $14,000 for a tomato soup can painting—to hang over his bed!)

Though *Bitch* was intended to be a paean to the couple and to spotlight Marie, Gerard and a little trick of Willard's, named John, join Edie after the first half hour as if swelling the rank will make cinema: but the deepening twilight of Hart Crane's "chained bay waters" is somehow more interesting than the five figures caught in it.

When the second part got off to a wobbly start, Andy bit his upper lip and turned to me and asked, "You want to step in?"

I do and sit on the back of Marie's chair and hold her hands comfortingly for most of the reel. We whisper together and she kisses me a lot. She appears to see me, amongst the unfriendly, as a friend and confidant, but I felt the interplay was too far off kilter for me to find a significant creative purchase. Marie roars, "Hey, are we shooting a movie?" from time to time, a bit of supposed deconstruction which doesn't work at all. And when she cannot draw Marie out concerning her pulling a knife on a black kid in the subway, Edie sublimates her impatience by throwing a drink on John. As an act of frustration and ill-conceived film interest on Edie's part, I quickly made a mental note of it.

When it was over, Gerard rubbed his hands enthusiastically and exclaimed, as he always did at the wrap, "It's great, man!"

But Andy, sitting with legs crossed, one elbow resting on his uppermost knee and his thumbnail in his mouth, just stared ahead and said, "No, it's not."

Then he broke his stare, looked at me, and inquired: "You want writing credit for this?"

I answered, "No."

What's interesting about this is that he considered my on-camera extemporizing to be as much a part of the work's scripting as the typed-up sheets I turned in without fail within a few days of his requests. Lacking a screenplay altogether did not mean for Mr. Warhol that the film hadn't been written. Of course, I was perfectly aware that these scripts were blueprints for myself, cribs, as it were, for when that Auricon began irremediably setting down the minutes for not necessarily friendly future eyes. That is one reason I labeled them "scenarios": they seemed to be that in a truer sense than those of most Hollywood films. I refused credit for *Bitch* because I thought little of that (never released) product and less of my small contribution to it. It wasn't because I didn't understand his perception of an independent film's writing, or find that intriguing, irresistibly challenging, or the skill-building opportunity it seemed to me it so undeniably was; nor, last but not least, that I wanted him to assume responsibility for this infelicitous entry.

Horse

A few notes in answer to questions raised recently concerning the history and details of *Horse*:[3]

Sheriff's repeated line to Kid, "Get out of town!" (e.g., Sheriff Pat Garrett to Billy the Kid), is an automatic, unresisted in-joke. Larry Latreille, playing Kid, was jailbait, a French-Canadian runaway who had fallen in with the Rotten Rita S-M drug groupies on the Factory's periphery, who often used the building's stairwell to shoot up. My accidental discovery of them one morning, along with their Factory tie Ondine's apologies for and explanation of their presence, led to my thinking about *Vinyl*'s mise en scène. The line is a half-humorous admonition and not so humorous (almost blackmailing) threat put to Larry, a not uncommon way of relating then among the Drella Dellas (Factory denizens). More taunting and gratuitous than particularly serviceable, it pleads the salon as the conflicted and competitive place Warhol-watchers claim he applied so much time to insuring would be always the case.

"To think I could have killed you a thousand times!" pops up in several scripts. It comes from the climactic scene in *Tangier* (Universal, 1946) and has no very special significance other than that I'd had a chance to study that heavily chiaroscuroed espionage film at the time, in theatres and on Connecticut TV, and that it was on my mind. Jack Smith made me repeat the line endlessly to get into character for a renowned still-photography shooting session. The

---

3 For further discussion of this film, see Appendix.

melodramatic cliché has a kind of representative quality: of melodramatic cliché.

Billy Name's extensive photo coverage of the *Horse* shoot is well liked and widely reproduced. Well-liked not the least for the coverage (sic) it gives to Tosh Carrillo stripped down to his jockstrap, a costume Tosh appeared also not the least uncomfortable cavorting in. It was Tosh's tush that brought an old lady to her feet at the film's Cinematheque premiere, and right out the front door vociferously determined to flag down a cop. Expecting the worst, stalwart Cinematheque owner-manager Jonas Mekas primed for action, telling me he'd have to confront the authorities if and when they appeared and let them know that art just isn't always pleasant; and that New York's legal division which regulates such limited activities actually must defend, protect, and further them.

When Andy, somewhat shocked himself by the dimension of Tosh's tush on the giant screen, and having sought a dark, private corner of the theatre to enjoy it, was apprised of the trouble to materialize momentarily, he rushed confused into the lobby, frantically seeking the guidance and protection of drug-mellowed Edie Sedgwick and her similarly mellowed guides and protectors. Failing to find them anywhere out front, the master panicked and ran to the street, where he discovered them all as yet unalarmed on a cigarette break; when he joined them, flushed with the NYPD news, they lifted their skirts as a man and fled into the night.

To lend variety to the films shot there, a different area of the Factory was chosen as the sound stage for each. Since the unexpectedly huge and tensed-up horse naturally arrived by the (much celebrated in song and story) freight elevator, it was thought wise to park it for the duration as close to that elevator as possible. Hence, the elevator and pay

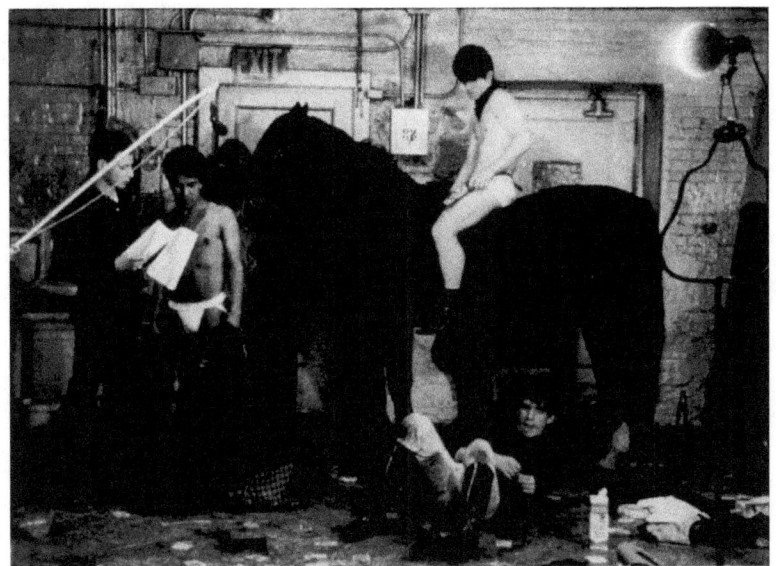

Ronald Tavel, Tosh Carrillo, Larry Latreille (on Mighty Byrd), and Dan Cassidy in Andy Warhol: "Horse" (1965).

phone to its left are in a way stars in this movie. But when Andy saw how the setup—the four young men in cowboy drag, the playing cards, pistols, other props, and Mighty Byrd himself—when assembled, so easily duplicated a Hollywood western, he was visibly perturbed. Wanting to disperse that realistic impression, he asked Harvey Tavel, the photographer Norman Robert Glick, and a third young man, a stranger (there were a number of thickly accented Italians at the shoot), to take up positions between the horse and the studio's east wall: in order not only to outline depth—the in-frame area became virtually a square—but to focus attention on the telephone and elevator. In addition, he asked the conservative-looking young lady holding the microphone boom to lower it into left frame, and Billy Linich moved the light board in to screen right. As a result, the film is notable for incorporating its own production. But a deconstructed (as it is) western is still, like *My Little Chickadee*, a western.

The line of silent witnesses headed by my brother so impressed me that years later I was to ask a company actor from time to time, but not every night, to sit quietly on stage and simply watch the play. While this was a common enough device in Elizabethan theatre, or occurrence if we assume the bodies were merely audience, I knew the perceptive in the house would see it as more than a classical embellishment. It is a dimension, depending on your mood, that either brackets a work in a way unsettlingly remindful of Plato's cave or, in a more contemporary manner, confirms the deferred reality even of what we see.

In regard to a staging of *Horse*—for this script would appear to be suitable to a stylized or highly styled, postmodern production—the Andy Warhol Research Project of the Whitney Museum of American Art asked recently why it never has had one. The simple reason is that the script was "lost" for years until a copy was recovered by Patrick Smith in 1978: at which late date I had no interest in recycling the scripts as stage plays. Another original turned up in the estate of Buddy Wirtschafter when he died.

The movie veers from the scenario considerably because of Mighty Byrd's unexpected size, and for reasons elucidated elsewhere; but that lends even more curiosity to a theatrical realization of this tract.

MoMA's restored print scores the movie's beauty as the original never did. Billy's spot placement, upper right, has the effect of a planetarium, clearer-than-real crescent moon; and as the film lightens to white in its final moments, the 16 mm suddenly seems to stretch into letter-boxed format to accommodate the Michelangelo-bas-relief-like look of the sequential males and animal unrolling from end to end in an unexpected and modern, shattering recall of Mannerism's equestrian dignity.

Vinyl

In the mid to late sixties there would be some speculation that attempted to explain World War II. Specifically, people thought to ask, "How could the Japanese and Germans have committed those atrocities?" But before I was to become familiar with these treatises—the best as yet unpublished—it had occurred to me that the relentless record of human behavior in the Factory's filmwork argued the projects as a breathing canvas on which to explore this big question and immediately notate the results. What would it take to get people to harm each other?—something clearly on my mind as one direct outcome of making *Horse*. Would you have to do more than ask them to?—inflict pain on someone else? In addition, I knew that the film would ennature itself—that is to say, I'd need not create the issue—with a serious irony: that an audience will look at real torture and believe they are watching something faked. Because, via commercial movies, we've been made to think torture and violent death are more dramatic than they are. But the torture in *Vinyl* is real, and it is leisurely.

That we had at our convenience the necessary means for dissecting torture was more than apparent in my access to professional sadists through Ondine's drug trafficking: some of his dealers happened to be, in a manner of speaking, moonlighting-wise, sexually so inclined. And then there was Tosh Carrillo, whose instrumental, not to say coolly detached and businesslike, dexterity in *Vinyl* brooks no argument. Though sexual topics were a priority for Andy Warhol, sado-masochism was not amongst his conscious concerns, and he later found it serviceable to disclaim any direct hand in the S-M metaphoring of both this film and *Hanoi Hanna, Radio Star*. He let the inspiration and responsibility for the matter rest with me. And if I were to protest when questioned—by the medical, the morbidly curious, and the plainly salacious—but most notably by the highly regarded Japanese playwright Shuji Terayama—about my personal interest in these practices and claim them merely aesthetic, would I not appear to doth protest too much? This, somewhat akin to the irony of watching *Vinyl*'s torture and not believing that's what you're seeing. So I've always held it the better part of valor to let the matter rest where he did.

Now, although Gerard had bared his leather Lifesaver in previous films, it was he who would provide the opportunity to deal with this something less au naturel—shall we say, vinylized?—subject matter: when he asked Andy to persuade me to adapt Anthony Burgess's *A Clockwork Orange* as a screen vehicle for himself. Though some critics have felt that *Vinyl* captures more of what this novel is truly about than the later, multi-million-dollar Hollywood adaptation, I myself really don't think it has an awful lot to do with the Burgess book. And preparing my script for the product to be something rather other than literally it, I'd say I'm lucky that it isn't.

But it is a successful film on its own terms. Gerard initially exclaimed, at the Cinematheque premiere, "This movie makes a fool of me!"; and he indeed is disclosed in all his naked ambition and uninhibited hunger for attention. But neither is palpably offensive here. His display, rather, is all too human; and his charisma, holding together the rambling proceedings, carries the occasional drop in pace quite nicely. Edie Sedgwick as a casual tormentor at screen

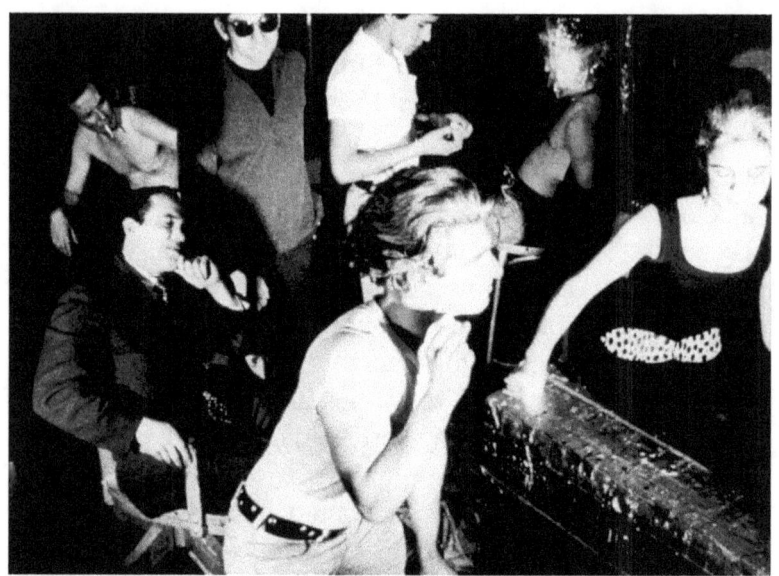

Gerard Malanga (center) and Edie Sedgwick (right) with John McDermott, Jacques Potin, Ondine, Tosh Carrillo, and Larry Latreille in Andy Warhol: "Vinyl" (1965)

right—tormenting by the mockery of insouciance and mime—is also an asset since her reactions as an actress to the torture are very readable throughout. She pretends to be too sophisticated to be disturbed in the least, but when torturer Jacques Potain persistently offers his sadistic services to her personally, she firmly, if politely, demurs. Ondine largely is camera-shy, but cannot conceal the relish in his desire—in fact, because of a personality conflict, absolute need—to deck Gerard; and then pull him up by his long hair like the self-righteous Joab displaying Absalom's head.

Whatever Gerard's reservations concerning *Vinyl*, he didn't let them get in the way of his promoting the piece: it moved to sleaze row on Forty-Second Street, and from there around the country and world. As a matter of fact, it is Gerard's self-promotion that accounts for how well-known the movie is, rather than its being, as it so obviously is, among the most audience-friendly of the genuine Factory filmworks. "Audience-friendly" is an interesting label for so actor-unfriendly an entry.

Harvey Tavel staged the script at the tiny Caffè Cino on quaint Cornelia Street in November of 1967 to standing-room-only acclaim. Mary Woronov played the doctor in his version, a charismatic singer, Mike St. Shaw (of "Hurry Sundown" fame), did Victor, and the dancer Raymond Edwards startled onlookers as a balletic torturer. All three went on to act in Hollywood movies, but despite their talents, as with the film version of *Vinyl*, this time the theatre audiences sat calmly by, confident that they couldn't possibly be watching people being really tortured inches from their very eyes.

Need I say *Vinyl* was translated almost immediately into Japanese and enjoyed Tokyo stage popularity?

Kitchen

To coincide with the opening of the flower canvases in France, Andy planned a trip to Paris, London, and Tangier that was to get underway on April 30th. He urged me to come along as a fixture in his entourage, and for the sake of my inspiration sponsored by and fiction set in the latter city, but I was in no wise ready to face returning to Africa. He also was hoping to get me and Edie, whom he suddenly invited as well, to more readily work together. But I, not yet understanding the extent of her familial crippling, habitual poor choices, and dependencies, believed the working relationship was smooth enough. We needn't be thrown at each other on a whirlwind tour, full of devastating memories, where forced shared time could only exacerbate whatever differences might already exist. Her grace and sparkling expression encouraged screenplays to leap quickly to mind: I couldn't complain. She had indisputable star qualities, I imagined she'd be more than willing to consolidate her energies to promote them. If I was aware of the wolverines lapping around her lovely edges with a slightly different agenda, I tried to look the other way.

While the helix of Andy's plans for Edie began to widen wildly in his own agenda during these weeks, he introduced me to his interest in making movies that somehow would impress the viewer as being entirely white or entirely black. In time, he would want one of each juxtaposed on a double screen. This concept had such priority in his thoughts, particularly in his ruminations related to scenarios, that when asked about his work with me years later he would respond by referring to his communicating with me concerning his innersight ideas on black and white.

He had understood, of course, by this point in his creative journey his cornucopic returns on double images; and the appeal of whiteness was unavoidable in the impression Edie was making then with her new look, eyes darkly highlighted to exaggerate her sheen-white face skin and hair cut short and dyed white to imitate his own wigs and pallor. Possibly he had seen in passing sound and cameraman Buddy Wirtschafter's wholly white kitchen in the latter's Soho loft.

Some of Buddy's former film students now re-work a picture of him as so heavy a drinker that he'd pass out right in class. But I don't recall him ever drunk when we had a movie to get in the can. He was on camera until May, and in charge of all technical aspects of the shoot that Billy Name didn't handle himself.

Kitchen is the first on-location lensing of the features I wrote, and images of that spring day remain brightly fixed in my memory. It was shortly after the entourage's return from Tangier, and Andy was kidding long-haired, questionably sized Gerard for being intimidated by the close-cropped and horse-hung Moroccans. Conceivably, the jolt forward in the authority of this screenplay (it is tooled to gutterize, and I think honor, Ionesco) was due to how even the suggestion of Volume Five of *The Thousand Nights and a Night* causes situations to rush to naughtied analects for me. Norman Mailer is associated with *Kitchen* because he was outside Buddy's building in the early morning to wish Andy good luck with the project. I remember him standing in the chilly street with a few colleagues as a kind of afterimage of Gore Vidal, similarly long-coated, businesslike, and pressed for time, meeting Andy for a quick briefing one colder morning near the U.N. (Much business, particularly of the networking sort, was conducted at the interminable night parties, but those terse and hurried, almost espionage-like, post-dawn encounters remain more vivid for me.)

Mailer attended the first private screening of *Kitchen* and, somewhat awe-struck, reviewed it for the Sunday *New York Times*: "It was a horror to watch... One hundred years from now they will look at *Kitchen* and see the essence of every boring, dead day one's ever had in a city and say, 'Yes, that's why the horror came down.' *Kitchen* shows that better than any other work of that time."

There are two schools of thought on *Kitchen* and a lot depends on whether you believe that what you are seeing is entirely intentional or not. Michael Silverblatt (KCRW-FM's "Bookworm") maintains it is all as it was meant to be, and that we are witnessing the disintegration of a production; Mailer imagines all of America to be disintegrating before us, and Andy, the most perceptive man in America, to be nailing it precisely. But if you think what you are seeing is not what was intended, however open and loose those intentions were, then you are trapped watching a cast that can't make one moment of an Absurdist-style screenplay work.

For the most part, they do get through that screenplay, the obviously fullest of my first half-year at the Factory. Andy wanted a vehicle for Edie that had situation but no plot (he was noncommital about whether there should be defined characters, cartoon-like characters, or non-characters), because, salivating Coastward, he saw the willowy socialite as his ticket to Hollywood. But because Edie is central to the frame and script, and because she expresses annoyance at being in the movie—irritation is actually the feeling most central to all her filmic appearances—she inevitably pulls the remaining cast, pacing, flavor, and experience of

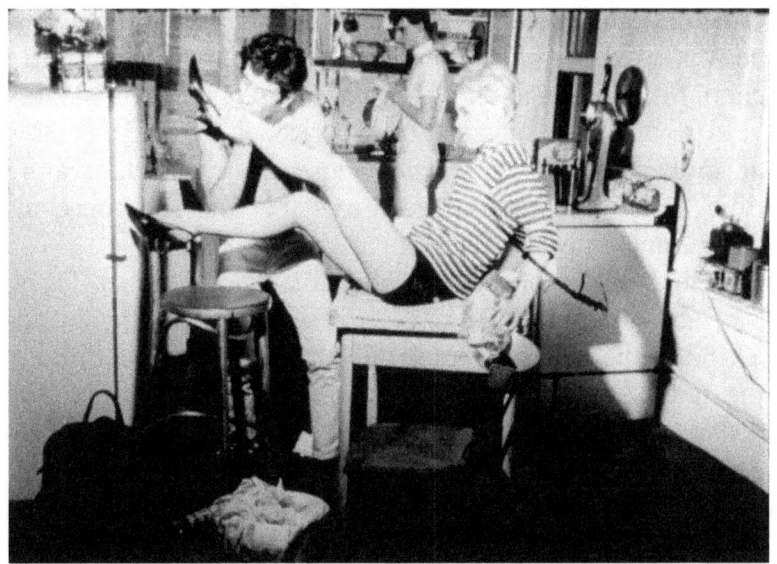

Roger Trudeau, René Ricard, and Edie Sedgwick in Andy Warhol: "Kitchen" (1965)

the whole in that direction. To me, she was more charming getting out of the cab that morning, her Nyoka leopard-fur falling from the one shoulder on which she always sported it, chatting about how Andy wanted her to take acting lessons but that if she couldn't learn by doing it, heck, what good would lessons be?

Kitchen was rehearsed for a solid week with Andy co-directing: we actually sat side by side on chairs Billy fixed up to closely resemble the cliché Hollywood fold-out with "Director" emblazoned on it. He was very fond of this script, and in keeping with his serious designs for Edie, had selected Roger Trudeau as a suitable foil for her. Roger was a tall and pliable masochist, drawn to the Factory by the shenanigans of the previous scripted film, and a kind of real-life Clark Kent: when bespectacled and in everyday wear, he appeared self-effacing, quite average, almost timid; stripped to the waist he was a stud for all seasons. So Roger seemed an attractive enough leading man for Ms. Sedgwick's Tinseltown bid; but her Harvard cheering squad and sly coach, Don Lyons (now an influential film critic), for whose casting in the feature Edie forcefully proselytized, gives the first self-conscious and mannered performance in a Warhol movie.

The addition of the perambulatory photographer, David McCabe, and René Ricard (ditto, an influential critic now) as a kind of speed-driven housekeeper, was to help get through the mollusk-memoried Edie's fumblings with the script. The delivery of the typed dialogue runs short of the proscribed seventy minutes of footage, and the crew comes in-frame to devour time by devouring the marshmallow props on set, giving us a chance to see who was there and what they wore that morning long ago. It also is the only instance of Andy and myself on film together—and in answer to the pressing question posed to me concerning that historic moment, yes, the shirt I'm wearing is vinyl

It was during the Factory trip to Paris and Tangier that the remarkable filmmaker, photographer, and architect Jack Smith approached me with a project of his own—to, as it were, keep me off the streets while Andy was out of town. Sometime in 1952, most probably, when he was twenty years old and living in Los Angeles, Jack had shot brief, melodramatic color sequences inspired by, and perhaps too imitative of, the treasonous multi-intrigues in the last reel of Universal Pictures's Christmas 1942 blockbuster, *Arabian Nights*. Smith's Technicolor is lush, varied, and commendable, but the camera work is dead-on frontal/confrontational and almost as stiff as the amateur performances of its youthful cast. Jack had been able to edit no releasable footage from this idiosyncratically uniform material up until this point, thirteen years later: but now suggested that it all might be scraped off the ash heap if I were to create intertitles for the canned product as it then existed, inventing a plot of sorts and "delirious" dialogue that could fit its silent action. He then, he swore upon a stack of Korans, would decorate each title elaborately with Arabian Nights Entertainment decals somewhat indebted to the title designs on the Universal movie—simple but beautiful scalloped pansies and violets, peacocks, leopards, and veiled harem damsels who, unencumbered by gravitational considerations, appeared to float joyously about à la Marc Chagall. I had known Jack Smith for some three years by then, and had collaborated on literary, film, and still-photo undertakings with him, but never before had he so tempted me with a proposal, snorting through his nasal as he did, that though the early title cards of silent films are obvious, tedious, questionably spelt, and composed as if for an all but illiterate public, they had evolved to near aesthetic respectability when, due to the coming to film of that boogeyman Sound, their bright future had been squelched underfoot—like a bunch of Arabian grapes. "—But!" he chuckled, choked, and chortled, inhaling on a hookah, "it has fallen to you, Ronnie, to scoop their discarded splatter up, and take the composing of frame titles to an Art Form!"

Aside from the fact that we obviously shared a demented passion for the Moslem East (now enflamed by Andy's junket), what screenwriter could resist so corny—and complimentary—a come-on? I set about the task with dispatch, an offering to be baptized *Buzzards Over Baghdad*, utilizing a vocabulary that was a humorous stretching-to-nearly-the-absurd of Sir Richard Francis Burton's imaginatively concocted epic-language for his Levantine translations, combined with Jack's own sense of colorfully exaggerated, psychotic, exotic, and beautiful prose. Smith and Burton shared a disconcerting habit of suddenly dropping into prosaic or contemporary scientific jargon that I found maniacally counterparting irresistible.

The "plot" of my intertitles for *Buzzards Over Baghdad* spins on the Caliph's reluctance to pardon a male slave's transgressions despite Duyazade's pleadings (e.g., Shaharazad's sister).

Now, depending on my schedule, I'd generally responded when called upon to serve as one of his "creatures," as he somewhat indiscreetly labeled them, but his invention for inducement in this instance wakens the watch—for something which he, as an accomplished writer, it would appear could do quite well himself. Consider the point in artistic time at which this takes place—I gave him the intertitles on May 11, 1965, with a promise to do more when the designs on these were completed—in other words, at the height of the truest creativity that Andy was to exact from me, just after completing the screenplay for and while rehearsing *Kitchen* and gearing up to write *Shower*. It argues that in our creative frenzies we give off an almost sex smell, intoxicating our neighbors or even downwind strangers, eliciting their animal need to get in our pants, metaphorically or otherwise, to get a bit of the action for themselves. But for Jack the appeal was a double gamble, unusually chancy, an intrigue also to be found in the Universal Pictures movie, where an army captain lacking foresight (played by matinee idol Turhan Bey) seeks not only to obey the Wazir's traitorous and sinister demand, i.e., to remove the Caliph's influential fiancée, but to fill his pockets at the same time (by selling her into slavery instead of putting her to the dagger, for which duplicity he himself is put to it). Because for Jack, this was not just a carefully timed opportunity to get work out of me, timed so that what would be forthcoming might well be prime, but an "Open, O Sesame!" to steal in the bargain—he'd feel justifiably—something from arch-rival Andy (whom he always called "Andy Panda"). Believing it would further his acting career, Jack had appeared in *Batman/Dracula*, a very early Warhol effort, and would act for him again, but he was not beyond tormenting himself well after the fact with the notion that Andy had vampirized him and therefore owed him aesthetically beyond calculation; nor above a kind of theft (for the nature of thievery preoccupied him) to insure that that incalculable debt would be paid. Jack Smith repeated a pattern of triangulation throughout his life, in which like a rutting steer he challenged a strong rival for a metaphysically symbolic, highly prized third party (the main plot, to be sure, of Universal's *Arabian Nights*). That the cross-relationship at its height of these two artists and myself could be introduced so sun-and-sand horse operatically into this compulsive, triangular modus operandi would prove too familiar, as well as far too film-like, for Jack to resist.

As luck would have it, for life if you'd so have it will resemble a Christmas blockbuster, our late nights together caused me to arrive late and slightly distracted for the *Kitchen* rehearsals, setting Andy's antennae upright; and so, no slouch himself at precisely this kind of possessive competition, he actually waited for an unguarded moment on my part, and disarmed me utterly by leaning forward and saying directly: "I don't mind you working for Jack Smith."

For the healthy stipend he afforded me, no? Yet more remarkable than the colossal nerve and astounding assurance of this Warholian territory-marking is the accuracy in his estimation that this surprise attack would pay dividends. For the Robber Baron of Postmodernism was a man I had also watched "cure" by the laying on of hands. When the crowded freight elevator stalled one day, a young woman grew rigid and went into formal trauma: without a second's hesitation, Andy all but sprang, put an iron grasp on her shoulder, and incanting beneath his hypnotic stare, brought her completely out of it. This mystic power is a power designated to one by others, true enough, but it is a real power nonetheless, and I had a very vital respect for it.

I was tongue-tied, and uncontrollably accepted his obloquy of my moonlighting as artistic treachery. I could feel myself grow hot all over, and swallowed and nodded and swallowed again.

And afterward, determining not to let this "superhuman" fully dominate my output, I nevertheless made certain my social or collaborative dealings with Smith were in dens off alleys on Amphetamine Gulch well beyond the master's ken.

And while the making of the grimly punitive *Hedy* the following year—in which Smith, curiously or coincidentally, would contribute a stunning performance, for he was an extremely accomplished film actor—will be read inaccurately as a kind of requital for the infractions of a subsidiary or two, it is all to a general annoyance and personal discredit that I, at least, ever saw myself, and consigned him the power to treat me, as a subsidiary. Jack took particular (and ironic) umbrage at this, berating me even sixteen years later, on my return from Thailand, with having "the same blocks," "always working for" someone else, rather than assuming the fugleman role which alone could steer me through the shallows of a gathering obscurity. But whatever one's to make of it all now, the *Buzzards* incident represents the high and touchiest point in what art students today call the Smith/Tavel/Warhol interdynamic. And whether or not Warhol saw *Buzzards* as my balancing his own side work with Wein and

Sedgwick, the rare and enviable imperative among us would never after be the same.

Finally, they not amenable to good common sense may find a (Great White Demon's) mystic retribution of sorts in Jack Smith's own guilt-related retreat here to his lifelong incompletion practice. He never designed those title cards for, nor consequently was ever able to construe, the pasty puzzle—and delirious pledge—of *Buzzards Over Baghdad.*

Shower

When a friend of Andy's, Aaron Fine, dying of cancer in September 1962, inquired why he chose to depict the Campbell's soup can, Andy answered, "I wanted to paint nothing. I was looking for something that was the essence of nothing, and that was it."

He also produced Campbell's soup can sculptures, exact-sized duplications of the food-containing tins, much along the line of the Brillo boxes that I so admired. One day during this conflicted period, a rather sweet, middle-aged couple was in the process of acquiring one of these tins when the wife, holding out a pen, explained that they really couldn't unless it had the artist's signature. "But I don't do that," Andy responded. The couple smiled, and persisted. Andy was watching me pace because I was waiting for him, a short distance away in the Factory, while the customers haggled. Then he summoned me, placed the soup tin and the woman's pen in my hand, and said, "Sign this with my name."

And all but coinciding with this incident was the distraction being provided by the erotic daring of some new shower-soap ads then blitzing TV. Andy was mesmerized by them: he told me he found them "really sexy" and said he thought "we should do a shower movie." Once again, the scenario was to be aimed at producing an entry in the all-white series, and was to be still another vehicle for the all-white female lead, Edie.

Although she believed I did not like her and ventured to put that in as many words, this spoiled brat and increasingly incapacitated substance abuser clearly was a muse to me.

But the time had come as well to take on the adventure of Pop-imaging The Nothing—which Andy had manned up to with the Campbell Soups—but which I had to tackle with English, action, two reels, a rickety camera, and our superstars—who I gambled might well suit the subject, since they appeared to have, in the quaint coinage of the day, "nobody upstairs."

S*hower* was written in forty-eight hours with one eight-hour break for sleep. I don't recall wasting time eating during that stretch. When I finished, it was evident I'd made some kind of breakthrough, that is to say, I was somewhere now I'd not been before in my work, in my life, in the Factory. Roger Trudeau, once more drafted to play opposite Edie, knew it at a glance, as did Dan Cassidy, who was quick to respond and line up for a role; nor was Andy slack in recognizing that something had happened here, an abstraction with sore feet. But I myself wasn't at all sure where to locate it: and was to make the mistake of trying (immediately) to repeat several times *Shower*'s confident gag-through in its customized, tense, and tailored English before finding that useless and striking out in a different direction.

Edie alone was impervious to what I'd come up with for her. Indeed, it was evident to anyone who cared to really listen to the woman that she had absolutely no idea of what Andy was after or had ever done, of what the films effectively were or what they effectively would be. If ever she had had the capacity to be involved seriously with art, her world was becoming confused now, and her hedonism, a poorly chosen safety vent, had risen to the fore and was monopolizing her day. She was exceptionally easy prey, then, to Chuck Wein's suggestion that she need not dilute her pleasures with memorizing scripts and rehearsing them, for he himself could furnish film ideas for her that used no scripts. Only Tavel was in the way: why not, he urged, dislodge him—tell Andy that you "won't be a mouthpiece for Tavel's perversities."

Sloppy with her sleeping pills and cigarettes at this embattled point, she accidentally set fire to her apartment and was seen in the papers being towed from a smoke-filled hallway, her leopard coat (all she could think of saving) askew upon a thin shoulder. Some jungle girl.

But she managed to memorize the one Wein line and be shrilly theatrical delivering it to Andy, who, not having her on salary, of course, thought retracting the talents at his disposal the better part of canning product and wasted no time with inutile objections.

As for myself, I was forced to acknowledge by then (June 1965) that Edie couldn't be a mouthpiece for anyone's dialogue, perverse or not, since she was completely beyond grasping the simplest stage directions, knowing right from left, in fact, let alone learning a role. Nor was there any point in my trying to reason with her, for in those days many actors believed that they should perform stoned: since acting, like any other activity, was something to be enjoyed. That it is a job was far from their thoughts, and the shaky chip fallen off the old social register was about to do anything but take a job in addition to the one she already had, that of killing herself.

Finally, Edmund Kean said, "Dying is easy; comedy is hard." And though ultimately opting for the less arduous task, Edie as a legacy confirmed that a comic's timing is the first thing amphetamines kill. A glance, which one ought to give it, at her conduct in *Kitchen* is, in the vigorous face of Andy's staunch amorality, a moralizing case in point.

So the filming of *Shower* was canceled; and at Andy's urging I proceeded to see to the staging of the piece and, in effect, the creation of Ridiculous Theatre. Andy wanted to lens the stage production of *Shower* on its second or third weekend, but the cast, some of whom were Equity members, naturally and correctly objected. After that, rights to the one-acter were sold to Off-Broadway producers, and all question of Factory interests in it obviated.

Ironically then, my best work under the painter's tutelage eluded his net, and though my debt to him for *Shower* is greater than for anything else, it is the one work he could not stamp faultily or make the least claim to.

If some people have regretted that we have no record of Queen of the Underground Beverly Grant's performance (in the role intended for Edie), or Mark Duffy's (of the Living Theatre), or John Vaccaro's, or the late Elsene Sorrentino's, not to mention Jack Smith's with its engineering setup for the showers, the work at least evaded the perpetual insult of an inadequate Warhol take.

Space

The new directive is toward total abstraction. This would serve several ends. By returning to the starting line, it would break the block that *Shower* was having on my imagination. It would circumvent some of the professional problems the recalcitrant faction on Forty-Seventh Street was creating for the filmwork. (That Andy had planted the seeds for and nurtured this rebellion was quite beside the point, though my equanimity in the face of it tantalized him enough to become a point of reference in his dime-store psychoanalyses of me with intermediaries.) And it would furnish a detour to what he perceived as a sudden jump backward on my part toward narrative.

This is the blueprint of *Space*:

The figure "8" is linearly the most complete and complex of the digits, and visually the most interesting; and the symbol of infinity, etc. Pursuant, there would be eight characters (or readers) in this movie, seated in bridge chairs arranged to delineate an "8." Each would hold a single page of dialogue with eight speeches typed out on it, some of them but a single line, others several sentences, still others exponents of these. All would appear to be abstract or so pulled from their contexts as to be coextensive with abstraction. People enjoying long memories will recognize snatches of radio ads or TV commercials current that July. Other speeches are snatches of conversation that I overheard as I went about town—accumulated much in the manner of the banter-gathering "Arbitrary" I'd devised for writing *Kitchen*. Still others are page-tapes of the odd way I was often hearing the most off-handed remarks, stenciled so as to preserve or attempt to preserve the illogical and idiosyncratic way I was hearing (receiving and processing) them. That is to say, that we sometimes are conscious of the silly, peculiar, or uncontrollably disrespectful associations we are making when someone addresses us in regard to the most perfunctory or innocuous affairs of the day: and a percentage of the dialogue in *Space* attempts to represent this experience. Occasionally, there are references to public figures or persons on the mid-Manhattan scene, and to then national events. I recognize most of these today, as well as the sources of the fragmented observations, but space (take the pun) doesn't permit investigating each, not do I think many would be edified if it did.

More to the art is the interesting M.O. intended for *Space*. Considering that it hints at the broad mysticism in vogue at the time, infinity, chance, the ordered and the arbitrary, Gurdjieff and Ouspensky, and the spatial nature of a two-dimensional art form (the previous films kept the problem of time foremost in the viewer's thoughts), the *I Ching*, another unavoidable fashion of the mid-sixties, would be called into play here to dictate its overall flow via physical movement and progression via the compass: the fact, or space, of the film.

Other than the looming reality of Andy's large hexagram paintings (the *I Ching* consists of sixty-four, i.e., 8 X 8, symbolic hexagrams indicating wise courses of action), the connection I made between the artist's ungiving aesthetic and a random throw of the *I Ching* sticks should be evident. By casting them, a mike-in-hand M.C. (or Arbitrary Hand of Fate) would be guided to move from character to character. When she brought the mike to the mouth of a character, that character would read a single speech from the dialogue page in his or her possession, canceling them out in the (*I Ching*-dictated) order in which I had typed them. To that extent, the fact of the film was randomed away from my own hands, from my instincts and inclination, which I deemed, as Andy's guide through *Space* here, was my duty adequately fulfilled. An "exploding image" might or might not await us at an eighth (or the forty-eighth) speech depending on exactly what dialectic had built to it. That an eye-opener ex cathedra only might be articulated made the prospective movie a party of the gods: and that particularly tickled me. But in addition to what I esteemed as quite comfortable enough aesthetic positions for a hot New York afternoon, the dent in the unmalleable in this process would seem to be apparent in handsome measure: we are dealing with "performers" who at this point on that hot July 18th afternoon will not or cannot learn lines, will not or cannot stop drinking and drugging for two hours, follow directions, or even remember to be civil. This unusual-looking scenario inconveniences them with no such unreasonable requests …

This is what happened instead:
      The fire that Andy had lit under Gerard in the early spring was smoldering now, and to extend the metaphor, in a space claustrophobic enough to fog and clog the latter's clarity and self-control. Time and again, Gerard enters in his diary evidence of the umbrage he took at the centrality Andy was giving to Edie and her own drone entourage (a segment of which *Space* is about to disclose and disclothe for posterity). Andy's placing her in a silent and peripheral, but strategic, role in *Vinyl*, a vehicle intended to concentrate on Gerard but which instead allowed the debutante nearly to steal his thunder, he tries to live with by telling me, "I didn't mind Edie in *Vinyl*: she kept out of my hair." He resists

interpreting his being shunted to the side now as Andy's getting back at him for never having perked his employer with sexual favors; or the increasing and often unjustifiable overburdening of him with duties and cruel incursions on his free time (Gerard was paid $1.25 an hour) as a shrewd repositioning of himself against his objections to Andy's good-timing and time-wasting with Edie and Chuck. Though much has been said about Gerard Malanga's morbidity and negativity—e.g., over-negative readings of what was going down—their feuding was real, and it erupted publicly and irrevocably on July 18th just before the shoot on *Space* could get off the ground.

From the top, one stepped into a general disarray. Dissatisfaction with the quality of the recent films (the fuzzy sound, dim lighting, overall graininess) under Buddy Wirtschafter's technical jurisdiction, a wide-eyed but technically adept maker of some budget TV promos named Paul Morrissey had been brought in to assist him. Tall, thin, and gawky, he stood to the side largely drop-jawed at what he saw that afternoon. I spent some of the pre-filming time on my knees next to Gerard, Buddy, and Kristy Keating (the M.C.) while they took my voice levels for the reading of the credits, which I always fed directly onto the track: most often spottily at dead moments in the movie, but which that day Andy had asked I do all together at the opening. (My voice checks in thicker than previously while the day's treacheries are trenched in my brow: I look ill and quite unhappy.) The Auricon had been set low, next to the accessory equipment, where I was trying to get a POV-take from its tripod since we anticipated that this opus would be boasting our first pan-lensing, and by the Master himself. Close-lipped and while I was not yet in solemn voice-over voice, Andy began shooting me, adding a note of discomfort and confusion—

viz., you want to look good then, but have something else to do. Addressing Gerard sharply, and proceeding to offer no reason for the discombobulation, Andy rolled the Auricon to the far side of the "8," flush with the Forty-Seventh Street wall, but at a considerable distance in-loft of it. During this relocation, the tug o' war between the two accelerated; embarrassed, I tried to shut it out. Suddenly it turned nasty, with the poet this particular outing finding it impossible to sit on his outrage. They exchanged fierce accusations, and Gerard took off to my left toward the stairwell, where he paused for a moment for the defiance of denouncing Andy (but not by name) as a back-stabber, and then exited, slamming the steel door behind him. Edie and Don Lyons, pleased by the row, and exhilarated, kept in place at this point. The six other "Characters" with speaking roles were assuming their positions, albeit rather rattled. Andy favored a pair of scalloped brown cowboy boots that year which clacked with an echo on the studio's concrete floor. I heard that clacking getting louder as I was correcting the spelling of names and looked up to see Andy swishing very determinedly across the Factory in my direction, ultimately to tower over me, the quaking incarnation of his fury at Malanga's bombast.

"Take Gerard's name off the credits!" he spewed at me.

This is one of my most uneradicable photo-impressions of the sixties: myself on my knees, a ballpoint pen and scribbled page in my hands, Kristy holding a mike four inches from my mouth, and Andy Empire-Stated above me, poised to javelin the ripe pettiness of his Obetrol-driven malice.

It set the tone for a verité of puerility that will (when the restored print is in full circulation) cause many to rethink their image of the Factory.

The positive in *Space*:

The most fortunate notion in the film is the initial centrality of Eric Anderson, a dark-haired, broad-shouldered singer in a Plains Indian, long-fringed jacket. At the time, Eric was considered to be second only in promise to Bob Dylan—who, ironically, was courting Edie's filmic favors just then, attempting to lure her away from Andy and into his own stable of groupie aides. Eric plays Character One and, selecting the second and fourth line-clusters during the film ("Rudolf Valentino was called the most perfect, etc." and "I wish I didn't cut off my hair"), he sets them to folksy song with a winning smile, a lovely tenor, and beguiling gentility.

Next to Eric in affirmative interest is the arresting, spectral torso of Roger Trudeau. Roger is stripped to his wet white jockey shorts, and his skin appears translucent—actually to glow, as is said of IV users—while his abundant axial hairs form an amazing mat over the eerie iridescence of his pectorals, stomach, and pubes. But Roger's face, seeming as if made-up, has the hollow semblance of a death mask, his features now unidentifiable, and this a mere two months on from his scrubbed, health-club look in *Kitchen*.

Among the Harvard pundits that ventured down on Andy's world that season—in addition to Arthur Loeb, Don Lyons, Edie Sedgwick, and Chuck Wein, that is—we glimpse the famous Dorothy Dean, seated far right on the crowded red couch, sadly unintrusive as she waits to factor in her speeches. I say sadly, because so much curiosity surrounds this woman, the *New Yorker*'s first black editor, a masochistically dissipated talent, a miscegenatious fag hag and lush with a riveting whiskey baritone, very difficult to psycho-fathom. Brion Gysin said she was the gratuitously tortured toy of the Cambridge predators: she'd fall in love with one homosexual after another, who'd indulge her, lead her on, and crucify her. (Dorothy's last and most celebrated lover was the blond beauty J. J. Mitchell. When he rejected her definitively, she went to live in Boulder, returning to New York only once, to vigil at his AIDS deathbed. I spent some time with her in Boulder, where Dorothy succumbed to pancreatic cancer a few days before Andy died; she, in point of fact, was buried on the day he died.)

To the occasionally spotted right and rear of Dorothy in *Space* is Danny Fields, a prominent rock producer now, at the time a wry, objective Warhol-watcher. In a sense, Danny was my only real intellectual refuge at the Factory, and though he claims he is totally lockjawed and immobile in *Space* because he desperately "was trying not to make a fool of myself," his footage gives us a rare peek at this jade and jade-eyed, unobtrusive, in-depth commentator on the scene. (By the way, his short-brow hairdo is an amusing reminder of mid-sixties Beatlemania.)

The mess:
Edie was rebelliously pre-programmed for the shoot by her coup-minded drones, who lusted after my job, and the confusion unleashed by the Warhol-Malanga incident caused her to advance precipitately. Shortly into the lensing, after stumbling on her opening speech, she lifted her script and tore it to shreds. Then, she unwrapped for our delectation what Chuck and Don, who owned her ear, had planned as entertainment in its place—Lyons trying to catechize her— in between assurances that she'd made the *Times*'s rundown that day of the New York four hundred who really lived in New York.

It's not until after her theatrics that Andy, on Auricon, picks her up—in what would become his signature practice, like porn cinematographers, of missing the best moments—

and what we come in on, to the alert eye, and despite all theory "establishing" the amorality of the Warhol oeuvre, is, in effect, an anti-drug harangue. For the very young lady is already past the peak of her beauty; and her eyes, flashing with hedonistic self-involvement, widen meretriciously as she oscillates her hoop earrings and continually is amused by the fact that she cannot absorb, listen to, remember, or even understand one phrase of the spoon-fed catechism. Lyons leans toward her lap with venal patience, himself oblivious to the naked preposterousness of the sequence. Eventually she tires of Lyons and moves over to Eric's circle where, like a twelve-year-old, she appears to be enjoying the song-fest; but she actually succeeds only in (aggressively) disrupting and destroying his improv and so robs the film of its unique chance to catch this interesting and promising talent in an instructively creative act.

Lyons's leaning into Edie's lap does indeed conjure up those images of drones preening and nibbling on the queen bee, for we have everything here in the frame except their femurs scraping goo against her sides and their gruesome tarsi in her pockets. But the most startling of the pilot fish she has hosted to the shoot is Ed Hennessey, whom Andy ultimately decides to cynosure, who keeps bringing up the food and drink he is downing and heaving it on the persons closest to him—as if this were just the quite most amusing thing in the world one could do during a movie.

The collective impression of the remaining cast, by the second reel largely peripheral to Hennessey, is of kids who can't handle booze at a supersquare, small town high school end-term bender. Tedious; and embarrassing.

In this novice outing as a mobile cameraman, Andy is more conservative than he shortly would be. He slides the Auricon leisurely from right to left, makes some pit stops, then returns. He searches for compound configurations including those offered by the Factory's full-length mirror but, as I said, manages to miss the most telling of them. On this, a lot of ink has been spilt—how unusual; how much the pop artist's eye it is; how it calls attention continually to the fact that we're watching a film (as if we could be doing anything but), etc.—but this column-fodder is simply the rationalizing that to the unanointed it always appeared to be. No film buff need feel intimidated by it. We also see the incubation of Andy's zoom-in, zoom-out work here. Mercifully, it seems only a tentative notion in *Space*, and has not the persistent irritation and idiocy of later opii like *Lupe* and *Nico and the Velvet Underground*.

So Kristy Keating with mike in hand and not the slightest semblance of cooperation from anyone around, or even instructions to direct her board-moves, moves about the playing area with no particular plan now, mechanically trying to pick up any partier at all who might extemporize something to say, read, or sing, since, to express my own disgust at this waste of good stock, I too had deserted the ramblings, but midway in the shoot—and, it is to be hoped, with fewer pyrotechnicals than Gerard.

So as not to lose all its material or the time invested in this scenario, and needing an abstract center-section in my play *The Life of Lady Godiva*, which I would write in three weeks in that coming September, I lifted a number of the line-clusters from *Space*'s unread pages and planted them there. The concept of a stage-route or floor map trigonometried by Infinity and an "8" would wait until 1984 to be utilized, when I directed *My Foetus Lived on Amboy Street* at the Theater for the New City, near the corner of

Second and Tenth. *Foetus* was a radio-drama written on a ZBS Foundation grant in 1977, whose "frank" material had doomed it to sparse air-play. Not willing to let this piece go at so few spins, or leave it to join the fate of *Space*, I adapted it for the stage, directing it in profile—a difficult process, but one I felt necessary to force me to rethink in nature its free-associating tale of woe originally intended to be comprehensible, and funny, entirely orally. Enormously aided by the long, rectangular, conceptual set of the late Ron Kajawara and the continuous wall-climbing choreography of David Semritc, *Foetus* unquestionably was the high point to date of my stabs at directing.

Interestingly, both *The Life of Lady Godiva* and *My Foetus Lived on Amboy Street* participate strongly in the miraculous—an aspect of this universe for which Andy, despite his daily prayers and weekly celebration of the Eucharist, showed no very noticeable confidence, disposition, or devotion.

Kahuna!

The shout-out in the political maze on Forty-Seventh Street brought a shakeup in the film personnel and, consequently, the direction the movies could now take. Uncharacteristically, Andy had gotten himself in over his head, and was finding producing two sets of films, one under Edie's brainwashers' orders and the other utilizing the old guard, a balancing act beyond his flexibilities, financial or otherwise. He was not yet ready to give up his leverage in my writing (the more conventional) scripts for Edie, nor would he ever be really until she left his life definitively, a year and a half later. He and I tossed about a few ideas; I showed him several sketches, some of which he found alien to his aesthetic and some of which I'd think better of letting him have. My allegiances and feelings toward him irrevocably mixed by now, I would not involve myself personally with Factory shoots until the following February. Nevertheless, decrypting Off-Off-Broadway's Machiavellianisms as not necessarily less volcanic than the Factory's, and needing to release the tensions in my first legit theatre experience, I decided to try to stockpile scripts and wait for things chez Andy either to make some impressive breakthrough or come to a sensible conclusion, e.g., any, from which one could proceed.

Some of my personal writing milestones at this point are additionally explained by the fact that I was becoming deeply involved with an artist I met, appropriately enough, in the Coda Gallery when I'd gone there to scare up a production space for *Shower*. For I rallied sufficient coherence to seed an odd encounter on an eternal beach (I was raised near Gravesend Point and Bath Beach) that would anchor, if not my emotional turmoil, that emotion as creative propellant.

At first, of course, I was stymied. And so flipped through a mental catalogue of motion picture genres in order to jump-start the juices. For the Factory more than accommodated "formula" flicks, viz., the horse-opera *Horse*, the soft-core *Vinyl*, and the absurdist, domestic-drama/pseudo-slice-of-life *Kitchen*. But it still being summer, and the insolent incaution and beauty of Hawaiian surfing having come in for a windfall of media coverage then, the Annette Funicello-Frankie Avalon beach bongo, blanket-party genre most preposterously clamored for attention. I did not here as elsewhere in scripting ask myself why psychosexually.

The screenplay *Kahuna!*, though seminal for me, as I say, never was filmed, and its surviving manuscripts pose some problems. For one thing, though all are written in my prescribed two sections, one for each thirty-five-minute reel, every copy of either is labeled "Reel One." For another, the styles of the two differ radically; they indeed appear to be for, or of, two different films. The briefer in format is perfunctory and of small art interest outside of its Carl Dreyer-cum-Kubrick patient image of a Man-in-Suit unperturbedly dining at a fully set table on the very splashy but haunted beach. However, the longer of the two is a mature tract, and though insidiously lubricious very firm in what it is doing; it is certain-minded—and, if I might, seminally ungiving.

Yet both of these undated "declarations"—which nearly two years later are incorporated into my final Warhol script—for different reasons seem to have been written at the same time. That is, mid-summer 1965.

Two lines in the briefer ms. will be shortly re-enlisted

for service in *The Life of Lady Godiva*: again, dashed off in my pad on East Tenth in September 1965, thus dating that one. As for nailing the longer, it has a title page proclaiming its prospective technicians and players as the full, standard film family in the third week of July: Edie, Roger, Gino, Gerard and Buddy, etc. The notable newcomer is Dusty Rhodes, fresh from her inconsequentiality in *Space*. Now, it could have been no secret by early August at the latest that Sedgwick as a star, and Trudeau and Wirtschafter altogether, were on their way out: Edie for being an unrepentant and unmanageable dope-fiend; Roger for being a buddy of Ondine's but not of Edie's and the current in-crowd, and into S-M and hallucinogens, or irremediably passive on-screen; and Buddy for being branded now a techie teacher not up to techie snuff. Researchers at Brighton University and the Whitney Museum of American Art claim variously that in August, or even mid-autumn, I seem blissfully innocent of these developments, indifferent, or politic in moving along briskly making (rather than taking) no note of the shake-up. The better part of my convenable energies right then, naturally enough, were addressed to the alteration in my private life and the birth of the Theatre of The Ridiculous (it was receiving mixed reviews but doing sell-out, turnaway business)—but it would be foolish to assume that I was so distracted as to be anything less than both wary and watchful of Warhol at that point: for Wein, fortified by his triumph with *My Hustler*, was hubris-ing that he actually could replace La Warhola himself: so Wein's headlong crash was imminent. As for continuing to credit-list and write for Edie, even I could not think that she, though torn by offers and advice from her lover, Kevin McCarthy, and from Bob Dylan, who was tireless in his deprecating of Andy—succeeding thus in further confusing her—even I could not predict that she'd make so many self-destructive moves. In fact, in defiance of the above, I never wrote better or more closely for her than in the longer *Kahuna!* ms. If you read Aqua's dialogue, listening to the pitch, projection, rhythm, phrasing, and general tone of Edie's voice as you know it from her vehicles in which she prattles ad infinitum (*Poor Little Rich Girl* and *Beauty #2*), you recognize that this is the very girl. Like I said, ours was an enviable while never ideal working relationship; and she, in the end, my fortunate incentive.

I'm giving this space toward fencing in a time frame for the writing of the longer *Kahuna!* ms. because it will find its, or an, importance now (on the page; and, presumably, for theatre historians) beginning with Aquarius's line, "Yeah, but lots of people don't know what their names mean." From there until the end of the script we have a solid, unbroken sample of the commercially free, 100% pure Ridiculous logic/illogic. I mean, the extended Ridiculous dialectic as opposed to the one-liner exchange that creates, by constituting, *Shower*. My brother one night said to me, rather sweetly, "There's no sense going to bed now, Ronald, you'll only want to get out of it in the morning." It was to replay and replead the resonance of this sentiment that I think I labored at the Ridiculous canon. To test its irresistibility linguistically, culturally, and traditionally—for this kind of thinking and its exact tone, both nonchalant and hysteric, has an unconscious history. Now it would be a state-meant of affairs. The reasoning of *Kahuna!*-Major with its seeming, meaning-deaf correspondent is precisely the reasoning that sees through (take the pun) *My Foetus Lived on Amboy Street, Gorilla Queen, Arenas of Lutetia, How Jacqueline Kennedy Became Queen of Greece*, and *Notorious Harik Will Kill the Pope,* etc. It is my primary contribution to theatrical dialogue, and it is what climbs, rung by wrong, the ladder to a Ridiculous vision. The surprise that awaits in this surfing scenario is how early, and quietly, it was articulated.

I can't remember the name of the Richard Benjamin-like fellow I intended to play Man in Suit (odd concept, that), though, peculiarly, I remember he lived in the then new high-rise on Third and Eleventh, and that I'd met him somewhere downtown. The prospect of being in a Warhol movie intrigued him at first, but when the internecine shoot-out delayed the filming as summer dragged on, he lost interest and I believe thought as well it would be unwise to have a permanent record of himself amidst such disreputable outcasts.

At this point, I batted around a number of alternative ideas with Andy, but none of these materialized into filmed projects.

Kahuna!, obviously, is the precursor to Andy's *Surfing Movie* or *San Diego Surf*, shot in La Jolla in May 1968. There he locked horns in a power struggle with Paul Morrissey over who really would "make" this film. Determined that it should be his, to answer the increasing critical press that he had little to do with the numerous titles bearing his name, Andy watched in dismay as the fledgling fascist set up a camera farther on down the beach and began lensing the same sea scene (with Viva, Louis Waldon, and Taylor Mead) as he was. Furious at a takeover attempt such as he'd never experienced before, perhaps the single strongest artistic step ever brazened against him, and directly to his face no less, Andy packed up and returned alone to New York—and the bullets of Valerie Solanas. When he fell, his film field stood vulnerable to Morrissey's permanent appropriation. Following his recovery, Andy, spiritually twisted, would try only twice, or so, again to make a movie under his own hand, and then give up.

Unlike the discarded script fragments written about this time, the sections of *Kahuna!*, in deference to their strength, ultimately were placed, separately, between the spirals of *Jane Eyre Bare* in a last-ditch effort to save them. However, since that epic wasn't lensed either, even this extreme measure failed. But they clearly comprise a distinct work. Carefully directed, a film version of *Kahuna!* would make a greater impression on the thoughtful now than in the vanguard- and objet-congested sixties. And what a pity that Edith Sedgwick (as the credits dignify her) isn't sparkling off the freight elevator to do it justice.

As for Wein, today he's into "channeling" in L.A., where he claims to have frequent chats with Andy (!), and is a procurer for horse breeders. You could say then that he's still at it.

O*ur Lady of Paris*: This outline may be recognized as a preliminary for the assumed imaginary screenplay I use as Mario's major audition piece in *Screen Test #2*. But here, unexpectedly, it is a step closer to reality. To be sure, Andy found the medieval tragedy to lie quite luridly outside all that his aesthetic stood for, and asked me to do that sort of garish and "deep purple" thing on my own; or with other filmmakers. But the recent musicals and the Disney cartoon feature based on Victor Hugo's classic make both this sketch and *Screen Test #2* visionary in their anticipation of its widespread current appeal. Many a critic has asked himself why, since *Notre-Dame de Paris* appears to come at us right out of left field. The convoluted yarn was an asylum of my childhood (e.g., "Sanctuary! Sanctuary!"), and the melodramatic plots of the two-act Ridiculous stage epics all bear its direct imprint. Surveys show *Notre-Dame* to be the favorite novel of the native New Yorker, male, reading public. Why? Perhaps because it is about male obsession: and that, to a host of out-of-towners, is what New York has always seemed to be about.

*P*iano: Eddie McCarty, Obie Award winner for Best Actor in *Kitchenette*, 1967, was a burgeoning composer and superlative pianist who died mysteriously at the age of thirty. We were close friends back in 1962, during a period when he worked as the house pianist for a children's theatre. I wrote *Canticle of the Nightingale* then for him to score. His theatre declined the stage piece, but it subsequently was performed in Sweden in Swedish, 1968, in Denmark in Danish, 1970, and at the Manhattan Theatre Club in 1972. The European productions seemed to have no trouble with it as an adult show, so when Andy asked me in the autumn of 1965 if I had any of my own already-set material "we" might film, I changed the rather precious title to the more Warholian *Piano*—reconceiving it as a kind of oratorio sung by the cast around an engaging pianist: McCarty—and offered it to him. Then I came to my senses.

It stays a stage play.

*I*ndira Gandhi's Daring Device: John Garfield's daughter Julie made a fine, very strong replacement for Raul in the staged version of *The Life of Juanita Castro* that September. I came to know her and her family well; she was a sultry, smoldering beauty. In October, having no problem imagining Julie as a subcontinental seductress, political or otherwise, I wrote *Indira Gandhi's Daring Device* as a vehicle for her, carefully crafting it so that the exact same script could be used for either a stage play or a Warhol film. But by the time it was staged, in September of the following year, Julie was no longer with the Play-House of The Ridiculous, and

I also would see no reason to let Andy have my material on which he had no proprietary claims for use as Factory films. *Indira Gandhi* became a major hit for the Play-House and a major international scandal that would lead, in the investigatory pressures, to my unofficial break with the Play-House in 1967. Since it always has existed only as a one-act proscenium piece, it comes as a surprise to most everyone that this succès de scandale incubated as a Warhol screenplay—and a valentine to beautiful Julie Garfield.

Hedy, or the Fourteen-Year-Old Girl

To those for whom escape was a crucial aspect in the silver screen's management of their pre-adolescent lives, particularly its rapid transportation to distant ports of call, Hedy Lamarr was no easily dismissed idée fixe.

Ecstasy, with the nineteen-year-old Viennese ingénue's infamous nude bathing scene, was heavily edited stateside and not seen by kids. But her roles in *Samson and Delilah, Algiers, Lady of the Tropics, Dishonored Lady, The Strange Woman, The Female Animal*, and, most powerfully, *White Cargo* inflamed the befuddlement of the small boy hiding in the dark movie house in megamodern, ugly-world New York—which he hated and feared with tearful suffering. In *White Cargo*, Hedy played Tondelayo, a "native girl." "That," my mother finally explained when I bothered her enough, "is someone who makes love." Put simply, escapedom offered no more elusive, remote, or excruciating mystery. Got up in the darkest pancake conceivable, in a halter of inflorescent print, with hoop earrings, conchshell necklaces, bangled bracelets, armlets, and anklets, barefooted and sloe-eyed, Tondelayo alluringly unpawed her blood-purple fingernails from the sexsational lobby cards that were at least as malignant as the film itself. Not that the racist tale of pride, privilege, and loneliness was asleep at the wheel, either: based on one of the most firmly cloven-hoofed astonishments of stage corn ever devised (Leon Gordon's adaptation of *Hell's Playground* by Ida Vera Simonton), every sequence, every moment is worth its weight in Cedric Gibbons's art direction and E. B. Willis's sets. Smoke-choked scow compositions and palm-frond-plated frames ensconce white rubber plantation appointees comatosed by solitaire, jungle rot, this fiery wanton's lashing whip—and treacherously spiked gin tonics! For when naive new husband Richard Carlson, monopolizing her for such incomprehensible domesticities as concern adults, begins to bore her, Tondelayo brews him daily doses of undetectable, I-make-it-hemlock-in-my-version, treated quinine medicine and hangs ten for the predictable results. Catching its frequent revivals, I could never get enough of wised-up former bwana-beau Walter Pidgeon forcing Tondelayo to drink her own fatal highball out on a backlot rhododendron trail in *White Cargo*'s memorable final moment.

So when Hedy Lamarr with $14,000 in checks in her purse was arrested for shoplifting shoes worth $86 in a L.A. department store on January 27, 1966, the siren was much on my mind. Four facts that fetch her came immediately into play: that her beauty was said to be the impression of her extremely rare, symmetrical face; that a recent face-lift had been a bit over-zealous in restoring that beauty—she'd looked all of fourteen years old to me on a TV show that season; that she'd been married five times up till then, and had paid off a few of her spouses to secure their divorces (impressed though puzzled, I'd be calling her, in my scenario, Hedy Mrs. Lamarr); and that she'd invented in 1942, along with composer George Antheil, a Department of Defense-recognized, anti-jamming, frequency-hopping torpedo-guidance device—making thereby the myth of the lovely lady scientist in the patriotic and sci-fi pics of her day a reality.

Kleptomania seemed a sad decline for a star too big for even top-billing in the fifties programmers that could have attenuated her career. Still, retired in central Florida now, she continues to be arrested periodically for petty shoplifting.

Aside from the fact that both Andy and I are members of the "movie generation" (they for whom Tinseltown created a mythology more meaningful than the Greeks' or the Bible's), the tie-in with Andy's shoe fetish is obvious. But I wouldn't overplay so blatant an underling's dig in discussing the celluloid saga with which I protested the taking of the actress into custody.

Hedy, or the Fourteen-Year-Old Girl always is referred to as the grimmest of the Factory's filmic output: cutting down or belittling the international star or Andy for their symbolic relating to footwear was and is altogether hors de ligne in the Ridiculous approach to diversity. Instead, this kidding of Hollywood and art-world royalty—clearly anticipating *Gorilla Queen*—enjoys a familiarity with both that appoints them their rank in the American imaginative family: as accessible and tempting to tease as our siblings, and as they, dead or alive, with and in us forever.

Appropriately, *Hedy, or the Fourteen-Year-Old Girl* is as far-reaching in its talent hunt as the Underground would get: for it boasts the best of the old and new Factory guard, and then adds brilliance borrowing from neighboring studios as it were. "Star-studded," therefore, is putting it mildly.

For all important creative purposes, by the end of legend-making 1965 the presence and power of the Harvard Group was extinguished; and just before Christmas, as if to replace them, Andy, through filmmaker Barbara Rubin, found The Velvet Underground at Café Bizarre on West Third Street. Lou Reed, elfin and electric, functioned as their lead, lead singer, and spokesperson. He was accompanied by the biker-guised guitarist, wild Sterling Morrison, an androgynous percussionist, Maureen Tucker, and the dazzling Welsh music scholar John Cale, on wired viola and bass. For a while, then, whither the Velvets went, the Factory would. Andy foisted a new solo singer on them, a German model and bit-part actress, the icy moon-goddess and incubating Nazi, Nico. The maneuver would make superluminary-to-be Lou Reed forever uncomfortable.

But the oddest addition to Forty-Seventh Street was a blonde prostitute with a jaw that lay aslant, one Ingrid Von Scheven, idiotically redubbed, but not reinvented, as Ingrid Superstar. She, in a gratuitous and I'd conclude questionable turn, was taken on as a cruel and revengeful replacement for Edie—she actually did look a bit like Edie might have had her face been sufficiently pummeled. And Andy found that perversely, misogynistically attractive. I did not, her reverse screen appeal eluding me utterly. Nor was it possible for the scowling tart to "act" since she barely could read. She was treated contemptuously by the Drella Dellas and returned just that and nothing more to the camera. Like the lady whose spikes she was deputed to fill awkwardly, Ingrid was a fierce dope fiend. She'd scan the Factory from the sunken couch as it were une maison de passe, and would diminish or destroy every role misfortune assigned me to write her.

But as if to compensate for Ingrid the Maladroit, Andy simultaneously presented me with a really cooperative and bright new light, a Fine Arts major Gerard had come across up at Cornell. He'd taken some test rolls of her and was eager to thread them for me. In the one I remember best, she wandered straight and tall into the soft sun, wraithlike or miasmic, in a field of swaying rushes, her presence as dramatic as the young Garbo's, and as strong. Her name was Mary Woronov, and it would be the actress's name that one way or another was to become most associated with mine throughout my life.

Harvey Tavel and John Vaccaro were negotiating a site for the then homeless Play-House of The Ridiculous, a narrow but high proscenium stage at 13 West Seventeenth Street, when Andy called me early in February. He claimed to have reestablished an atmosphere uptown in which I could work seriously, and said I was sorely needed for a script that would feature himself as cinematographer and show to advantage his latest discoveries, among them Mary (he'd hight) Might, Ingrid, Lou Reed, The Velvet Underground, and a bevy of young male hotties, hailing from Sunset Boulevard to Miami, Oklahoma, whom I was never to get quite straight or tell apart, neither in *Hedy* nor the two flicks that followed it. Someone I did get straight and could tell apart was Danny Williams, a bespectacled, short and husky preppie arriving rather late and lame from Harvard, for he'd become Andy's very odd whipping boy and peculiarly passive lover. He was a sound and light man.

Andy also had three refreshing suggestions, calculated to tempt me from my wariness. One, that he had learned that the upper floor of the Factory's building was a furniture storage loft that could be let for a day's shoot: and now, wouldn't that be nice? Two, understanding my frustration writing dialogue he couldn't get his stable ever to learn, mightn't I try simply conceiving whole sequences, instructing the performers on where they had to get from top to close of any given sequence, and then letting them improvise the rest? And three, mightn't I mix the new talent with old hands whom I knew and got along with well myself, because they'd cotton to what I wanted, be somewhat used to it, and able to acquit themselves professionally?

Generally speaking, unusual halcyon days were holding

on both the Upper and Lower East Sides. I had reason to expect good things from my forthcoming stage play, *The Life of Lady Godiva*, Andy with an entourage overhaul expected a new lease on cinematic creativity, and Jack Smith, drifting in his directorial aspiration, expected an appearance in a Warhol flick just then would do wonders for his "acting career." And he'd have no objections to pillaging his own stable for cast company. The scene was set for some interesting, if not sensational, work.

Hedy is divided into four easy-to-follow acts. Their settings are the Frankensteinian laboratory for the international star's over-wrought operation, the department store where she shoplifts and is busted, her stolen-goods-cluttered apartment where the arresting policewoman gathers further incriminating evidence, and the courtroom where she is tried, convicted, and—gulp!—executed.

It was a foregone conclusion that Mario Montez would play Hedy. Frankly, I don't remember why. It seemed obvious that Mario was the one creature around to impersonate a diva if that's what you had in mind. In retrospect, he doesn't seem so hands down a choice. He is sluggish in the first act because, once again, he is so interested in looking right or ghoulishly glamorous for the camera (it's hard to decide which), or is just so plain taken by being in an uptown big-screen flickeroonie that he forgets he has a whole logical sequence to get through, with essential lines and activities, in approximately seventeen minutes. You can hear me prompting him at painful stagnancies, not only with key lines, but warnings that that will be quite enough of that—like, stop standing around there and posing!

Tellingly, my voice is measured, relaxed, unworried. And Mario improves as he goes along. He sings, "I Feel

Pretty, Oh! So Pretty!" to mark the close of the opening act, showing that I conceived of *Hedy* as a musical stressing its book, and was forerunning, thus, many Ridiculous epics.

The Velvet Underground took their test trial, and trial by fire, of movie background music with utmost sincerity. They stationed themselves against the loft's east wall, not far from Andy, who—amazingly, unforgivably—never had the presence of mind to include them in his roving lensing. But they ignore the slight, and having quickly deduced that there were ominous aspects to the Hedy Mrs. Lamarr saga, privilege us with a foreboding overture, a meld of Stravinsky, Berg, and Schönberg: but it most of all is La Monte Young, a direct influence on Cale, and on myself since meeting him as a teenager. Then, when Lou saw the darkly lit operating room, closely resembling Universal's wartime Karloff and Chaney horror labs, he coaxed the group into a highly threatening but totally postmodern sound surround.

Lou was an innocent twenty-one-year-old from Brooklyn, fascinated, nearly hypnotized by the loonies for whom he was scoring. He'd become celebrated as the defiant, brazen balladeer of a mass-perceived depravity, of New York's smack and S-M dens, but it was strictly as a documenter. The Velvets' work here is both prepared and improvised; paying close and somber attention to the lines, situations, and physical movement, their composition is entirely noteworthy in its own right.

Arnold or Uncle Pasty, a heavyset, middle-aged fixture in Jack Smith's roster of actors and aides, whose dream it was to do yeoman service in artsy nudereenos, plays Herr Operating Doctor. A complicitor seeming to emanate from nowhere plays against him as his chatty assistant (referred to as Hans, of course), and the twain form a kind of Abbott and Costello team that challenged my authority to order them off the sound stage—in the grand, Elizabethan-clown stage-hog tradition. Ever vigilant to the needs of the drama, Jack Smith breaks in upon them in an effort to get them off, decrying, "You clumsy fools! You know that you have both been debarred from the medical profession!"—and then proceeds to take a surgical hand in the sculptural cosmetic himself. The act climaxes in a congestion of indulgent and-then-some hamming, while you hear, as I've said, both Andy and myself urging the cast to segue into the department store.

Now, I was intent on bringing to *Hedy* my childhood's deep and lasting scar involving Tondelayo's distribution of tainted tonics to studs currently in her way, in order to get expeditiously on with the unsampled novelties destiny must be stashing surely for her distraction. So, besides the off-key song, my scheme was to punctuate the act-ends with a repeated motif, by having Hedy get the inconvenient witnesses in each to cough back a draft of the tasty and terminal concoction. In Act One, she'd like no tattlers on her face lift, like a pharaoh wanting no pyramid-builders with detailed knowledge of his gravesite making the old Egyptian scene after his burial. Therefore, the script calls for Hedy to have success in convincing the surgeons to quench their thirst and lives. For some reason, I had trouble getting Mario to understand this plot-ploy's significance (let alone its reference to *White Cargo*), and that accounts for a deal of the confusion and whispering near the end of the first act.

But I had even more trouble getting Ingrid to remember it at the close of the department store bit. Ingrid plays a countergirl in the Bloomie's wannabe, whom Hedy attempts to distract while her henchmen remove all the artifacts— beds, chests, a sofa and vanities, etc.—under the countergirl's consignment. When the salesgirl outsmarts her by spying the hoist, Hedy urges the latter (a closet lush) to dink the quinine mix; but Ingrid staunchly refused—against my directions. Indeterminable Mary, as a store dick (!), busts Hedy; but I had to intrude onto the set, crawling all the way, to tap dumb Ingrid on the leg and remind her of what to do. This crawl beneath camera-level intrigued Andy, who had absolutely no idea of what my sophisticated story was all about, so he decided to dip the tripod and record my entire obtrusion. Startled, nay, dismayed, I was forced to drink the hemlock myself, like Tondelayo, and die right there. Andy, dear that he was, left the tilted camera on my corpse for a long while.

This transaction, entirely misconstrued by theorists/careerists, has come down to us in film classes as a sensational example of "authorial intervention"—the screenwriter appearing on screen to take (deconstructive) exception to the screwing of his script, to "die" symbolically as an objection to, and representation of, the painful passing of his pages. Actually, the misinterpretation began with the Philistine Morrissey, who was present as a techie and seemed to think that that's what he was seeing, and ever since has enjoyed retailing it. This is consistent with his understanding of everything related to Andy's work.

In Act Three, Mary carts Hedy over to her apartment to search it for what she suspects she'll find there: a treasury of hot goods. Here, our on-location furniture warehouse came in even more handily than it did serving as the Bloomie's set, for there is something dizzily hilarious in a star's lifting a lot of large furniture pieces. In addition, Hedy's home set sheltered yet another hidden reference to Andy, double-dared right under his nose. Specifically, to his own trove on Lex, several rooms of which held huge antique furniture.

To elude the nightly lockup, Hedy seduces the arresting dick on a conveniently stolen love seat, and this allowed me to introduce one of the all-time ultraconvoluted, male sex fantasies, that of getting into drag to bed down, lesbian-like, a tough female beauty. Following her knocking off a piece of nookie, the dick hauls Hedy off to jail anyhow—"just like a cop."

Hesitancy surrounds the use of the word "booster," which was common slang for shoplifter or thief in those days, or so I thought, for it appears to give the whole cast problems. Mario seems to remember that I told him to pun on it, as in "cheer-leader," but his delivery, disconcertingly, suggests that he really can't think of what else it might mean. In fact, the most interesting idiosyncracy that *Hedy* identifies is that, as Hedy Lamarr's appearance of guilt grows, Mario, in the manner of *A Double Life*, makes gradually no distinction between what is happening to himself and to his character. There is no question in the trial scene that he believes he himself is being accused of the character's immorality, fascist consortings, klepto thefts, briberies, lies, and payoffs. His involvement is the mirror of his soul: told he is obviously guilty, he becomes, to his distress and ours, defenceless.

The trial is the formal finale. As in the most conventional of dramas, a major character is introduced at this point to shape up the plot and put a bow on its tail. Here he is the judge, interpreted by Harvey Tavel in a tour de force twenty-minute improv. He tears through Hedy's five husbands with such velocity and vehemence that while grilling Husband No. 3 he breaks his gavel. Andy selected the chic heirs, and superstar hopefuls, who'd essay the spouses, and Harvey interviewed them one by one in the Factory toilet. He recalls there was so much commotion in the whole building, the only private place was the head downstairs. And once inside, to his amusement, the prospectives, outvying each other for a demeanor both jaded and pampered, had difficulty maintaining their dignity. He cracked: "I would say they had trouble keeping their noses in the air, but in there they had to."

Once again, Gerard wrangled his way into the movie in progress, so he plays Husband No. 1. We infer No. 2 is a drinker and card shark; that No. 3 has come starry-eyed to a Warhol flick all the way from L.A.; No. 4's daddy has oil wells in Oklahoma; and that Husband No. 5 is a poet with an Upper East Side nasal who fancies he looks like Emily Post while Hedy Lamarr's a dead ringer for Robert Browning, though the possible naughty plays on that name elude his "velly" superior blankety-blank.

To our everlasting consternation, Harvey convicts Hedy without benefit of jury and sentences her to drink the hemlock. This, of course, is Walter Pidgeon giving Tondelayo a dose of her own medicine. But it is the fatality of this poetic justice with which the surprised are abruptly left. Is that sentence, carried out before our eyes to the accompaniment of the Velvets at their most menacing, too harsh, too un-American, too unbelievable—or is the star system some kind of criminal give-and-take-too-much of which we've been not sufficiently conscious?

When Mario hears his sentence, he tells Harvey that he must "change for this important occasion"—repeating a routine he already went through when Mary let him know she'd pass on that tonic and that he'd have to be booked at the station. What Mario is trying to approximate (clumsily, arcanely) is his namesake's response to learning she'll be booked on suspicion of murder and searched for a stolen diamond, in *Tangier* (Universal, 1946). This gives La Montez a chance to get into a Travis Banton creation, a startling black hat and gown, but also the time to ditch that diamond amongst the ice cubes in her cocktail, which she asks the arresting commandant to hold for her till she returns.

The Velvets respond to the metaphysical overtones of Hedy's wardrobe-reaction to her arrest with a riff that extends through and covers the dead spot or silence of this costume change: a lyrical riff, nothing short of enchanting. In other words, if we waver between seeing this as a foolish transvestite's flippant dismissal of a charged disaster, and a charged-with-meaning correspondence to the disaster, the Velvets don't: they seize the second possibility. When they witness the entire perplexity repeated to stall her execution, they fall in heavily with a cautionary dirge and requiem for us all.

I signaled to Harvey that he still had two or three minutes of footage following Mario's expiration, so he calls Jack Smith to the stand as a kind of summary, post-mortem character witness. Jack had been "reacting" magnificently as a "friend of the court," his eyes narrowing and darting with deep concern, nay, agitation, from quizzer to testifier. He assumes the witness chair, or hot seat in this case, unable to articulate for several dramatic moments, so choked with feeling is he. But under Harvey's patient coaxing, he finally intones: "She was tragic and noble." Then, suddenly, the film ends.

What he went on to say, sadly unrecorded, is: "She had the face of a fourteen-year-old girl, the mind of an eighty-year-old hag, and the emotions of a mollusk."

Altogether the most talent-crammed feature delivered by the Factory, if *Hedy* has any major weakness it is Andy's cinematography, which, true to form, wanders aimlessly through much of the furniture missing the fare.

To conclude on a brighter note, on March 10, 1997, the magazine *American Heritage of Invention and Technology* honored Hedy Lamarr at a ceremony with a Munitions

Invention Award. Her son accepted the belated recognition and she herself, at eighty-three, spoke over the phone to express her heart-felt thanks.

Withering Sights

Something happened at the filming of *Withering Sights* that redefined my relationship with Andy Warhol, and altered it forever. He had to be made accountable for the incident, and that account put our work on track with a pointless destination.

Andy told me that his two favorite novels were *Wuthering Heights* and *Jane Eyre*. But since he would refer to them only with the names of the Fox and Goldwyn stars who interpreted their Hollywood versions (e.g., "the Leslie Howard character"), I had no reason to believe he'd read either. He had difficulty reading, and George Abagnalo, a teenager who worked as a general aide and budding writer himself in the Factory from 1968 to 1976, thinks he may have been dyslexic. Historians discovering books in the time capsules Andy left as part of his legacy assume he read them, or that they were favorites of his. Both assumptions want proof and are foolish.

What is certainly true is that Andy felt re-energized early in 1966, he'd regrouped his troop, rescheduled undertakings, and gotten back to the grind. High among his projects were his own cinema treatments of the Brontë sisters' sagas. But in March the stable of Warhol-exclusive performers was in disarray, and that both cramped and freed up my style. What I mean is that I'd found it easier, and faster, to write if I had actors to visualize for the roles. Seeing them moving about in my mind's eye just a few feet in front of my typewriter, as it were, made the scene more concrete for me and expedited the task. Having no one at all inspiring to write for, perhaps predictably, was to open unexpected vistas.

Ondine and Mary Woronov—she detested the Warholian subjugation of "Mary Might" as I did the diminutive "Ronnie"—were two potential headliners; but at this point, taking a fancy to each other, they were off together doing more dope than drama. So I was stuck with Ingrid Superstar (so called largely to mock her), the actress I could abide least in my life; the word "stuck" is repeated twelve times in the *Withering Sights* scenario. Of course, it is a tale of persons somehow stuck with and to each other over two generations, so in that sense the Maladroit, willy-nilly, tells the theme well unconsciously, and in a way that William Wyler, using Merle, never could. I remember looking at Ingrid and thinking, "I've been spending too much time lately with the beautiful superficial people. That has to change: I've got to spend much more time with the ugly superficial people."

Now, we had a twenty-minute audio of an ash-brown-tressed young man, anything but ugly, one Charles Aberg, discussing his very sixties self; and I wanted, or was encouraged, to incorporate it into the flick as voice-over while the fellow frolicked (or moped) about as a depressed Heathcliff. Since it would get me through twenty minutes of the second reel without a depression equal to Heathcliff's from helplessly watching all those competents not know what to do or say, I jumped at this time-chewer. But in the chaos of the afternoon's gross unprofessionalism, even that pre-recording went unused; it is of course long gone; and I've not the slightest recollection of how it went. A comely comer named Susanna Campbell was to play Nelly Dean in this mimed sequence, for Miss Dean, the narrator of the novel, does not otherwise appear in my scenario—i.e., the Brontë narrator appearing along with, as if doing, the Aberg narration. But we have no further trace of what was intended here as the sequence, however jarring to the work's main body, for better or worse, never was realized. But then again, neither was much of my scenario.

To be sure, a general attempt—shot to appear as if it were our initial intention—was made to have Susanna read through all of the dialogue while the assemblage tableaued it, they being too inept to dumb-show their way through under the reading. But in the end, this last resort seemed half-baked indeed and too crappy to stand by, or for.

There was a lovely woman who lived at the Dakota at this time, No. 1 West Seventy-Second Street, named Panna Grady, who was a patron of the arts. She had given the Play-House of The Ridiculous a small sum to launch its early projects (in March, *The Life of Lady Godiva* was in rehearsal), and since her suite at the Dakota took advantage of its Gothic look and nineteenth-century construction to develop a nineteenth-century feel, it was natural that Andy would ask her to open the premises for the lensing of a Brontë story. (At a subsequent use of her rooms, the Warhol entourage, led by René Ricard, trashed the place, not only ending Ms. Grady's involvement with Warhol, but spreading bad word about the Drella Dellas from CPW to Beekman Place.)

My own standing with the artist during the late winter and spring months of 1966 called for a justification as well, which I procrastinated undertaking until he finally forced my hand. As always, the day-to-day dealing closely resembled a familial tie: my presence and my work, when requested, were taken for granted. One might assume that by April my true fidelity lay in the theatre, but when we remember that I took playwriting, during the run of *Godiva*, no more seriously than I did screenwriting, that would be inaccurate. No, I still was waiting and looking for someone to publish my novel. And I'd wait for that someone, actually a gentleman, Maurice Girodias, until 1968.

With its importance easy to overlook, the most identifying exchange perhaps between Andy and me was his giving verbally at several shoots his full permission for me to refilm my screenplays myself as my own works, or have someone else direct and shoot them as theirs, after he had. This green light made no impression on me at the time, for who else would want these scripts so conscientiously tailored to his aesthetic, as I understood it, and current need? And why would I reshoot them, whose ambition was not to be an indie-maker? From today's vantage, we more nearly appreciate what he was suggesting, for there's always been time and footwork in store deciphering the puzzling pronouncements of real avant-gardists. First, he understood that his use of my screenplays was but one take on them, and that any competent other's might be equally valid, or end in a finer product. And two, he was implying that the core creation, in this case the screenplay, be recycled—an indefinite number of times. In this, he was not exactly forerunning the pathetic fashion of recycling so much as submitting to, and submitting altogether, the notion of what recycling in its true and best sense means: that there is no legitimately defendable definitive interpretation ever of a core creative work, and that we have never really done it right or well or else we'd be saved. And that, surely, we are not.

Andy would have understood the theatre staging of the screenplays—the first, *Juanita Castro*, by then already history, the second, *Screen Test*, to premiere early that September—as the screenplays' first recycling. (And this writing now as but their latest.)

In the meantime, waiting a more embrasive illumination,

Andy's biographer, Victor Bockris, claims an event just prior to my writing of the 1966 scripts explains that darkening clouds were gathering about me. It is only a theory with a certain purchase, mind you, I am not dishonest in telling Bockris, and others who ask, that I felt nothing odd or even very changed as the new year began.

This was it: back in November, Andrew Sarris, the undisputed "only serious" widely read film critic of the day, inadvertently caught a showing of *The Life of Juanita Castro* at the Filmmakers' Cinematheque, then in the basement at 125 West Forty-first Street, when it was substituted at the last moment for a flick that may have caused police intervention. His initial reaction (November 11th) was to call the work "an unheralded masterpiece" and say that he needed more time to reflect on it, and so would review it fully at some later date (how often does a critic say that?). Accordingly, the expansive notice appeared on December 9th and bore at its center these sentences:

"The creative force behind *Juanita Castro* is not so much Warhol, actually, as Ronnie Tavel, who wrote the script and acted the key role of the stage manager, and very good he is in both capacities. What is curious is that Warhol has assumed the role of mere metteur-en-scène..." So far as Bockris is concerned, from that Wednesday on, my days chez Andy were numbered.

I had trouble figuring out which baroque lift or spiral stair would take me up to Panna's, and so was a bit late to the shoot on *Withering Sights*. Her suite was thronged with extra extras, fashion editors, guests, and morbid curiosity-seekers who caused a delay in rolling Reel One anyhow. The parlor where we would film was smaller than I'd have wanted and worried me, since the scenario highlights a ball. Having been to a number of the patron's soirées, I wasn't sure why I hadn't remembered the sizes of her rooms better. A bevy of twenty-something male lovelies was gathered for this "cast of thousands" entry, rather difficult to distinguish from the husband-team in *Hedy*, no doubt because a certain culling of same was repeating here, again in throwaway roles. Ingrid looked smug and so more discouraging than ever, but annoyingly calm and self-assured in the centrality that her dual lead, as Catherine and Cathy, had placed her in, unearned. Cross-legged on a chaise, she in fact seemed, like Zola's Nana, to be receiving.

A friend of Andy's of several years' standing, a Shakespeare scholar named Paul Bertram, then Dean of Graduate Studies at Rutgers, had arrived at the Dakota to pick up Andy and spend the night with him on the town. Since the shoot was late wrapping, he had to wait in an antechamber and kill some time. To do so, as any English professor might, he picked up a spare copy of *Withering Sights* that happened to be out there and flipped through it. I heard some laughter through the foyers; then, wearing a suit, he entered from the antechamber smiling broadly and asked to be introduced to the screenwriter. I was sitting on a divan at the farthest reaches of the suite: I stood, pleased, I suppose, and came forward. But with startling decisiveness, Andy took Ingrid in tow and blocked my way, literally coming between Paul and myself. "Oh, uh!" Andy began tensely, "why don't you interview our star, instead? Paul, this is Ingrid—Ingrid Superstar!" Paul executed a graceful step back and, to spy me approaching, another half-step to the left, and responded with, "No. I want to talk to the screenwriter."

Then I took the initiative, circled around Andy and Ingrid to get past them, and offered my hand to Paul. He clamped down on it and shook it powerfully, complimented me on my comic take on Brontë, was as a matter of fact exuberant, I thought, and all at once started to laugh again.

Professor Bertram phoned me the following week. We got together, found we had a lot in common, became close for years, and are good friends to this day. Oh—he wears a suit everywhere, every day.

As for Andy's world-class show of his hand, it was one of those disclosures that the most reticent of persons must call to account and make the discloser responsible for, or always after be treated as the flunky he so blatantly is. The apprenticeship was nearing an end, and he'd make an uneasy equal, if indeed he'd make one at all. History would prove him an evil collaborator. For as true friend, equal, or partner, one would have to be accountable oneself for the man morally that he was, living in approval with the repercussions of his icy opinion, his selfish decisions, and the hoarding tone which he set that had to shape, if not young America, everything he himself touched, a life-style and tone whose aesthetic transcendence would never subjugate the infection of its greed or the outrage of its ethical indifference.

The question, then, was how much more he'd have to teach me in the most immediate sense. Meaning by immediate, in its proximity to its object and also as soon as possible. To repeat the obvious, sense and pride if not one's confidence in oneself harped on time as of the essence here. My work previous to 1964, as much as in whatever I did for him, spells out how I came to his door with a fully articulated sense of art: he knew that, he intended to make money from that, but he did want to give me, finally, something on which a price could not be set.

The screenplay of *Withering Sights* is bread upon the water, for its returns were proverbially postponed. A long-term profit was hidden in how it seems joyfully impervious to the hard reality that there is no way that the current Warholian crew is going to learn or do this. That being so, it is off on its own Freedom Road—to what? To the making of an art of self-indulgence and the apparent loss of discipline, to a sniffing out of extremities, a kind of frantic dramatic rushing that I wanted to, and would often from then on, be doing. *Withering Sights* in itself resembles a TV skit—albeit, cable TV, Bravo, perhaps—as free to find fun in, and poke fun at, everything without the least caution for how arcane the references might be and obscure the triple-entendres; or, on the other hand, how naked, obvious, corny, or low-brow. For whatever's recondite, that "skit" is a demonstration of how to care not; and for its trashiness, how to redress it. Or, undress it.

And the Master/Monster, to be sure, would very shortly have one more lesson to teach, or, if we undervalue him, direction to point me in, rich with expectation. But of all unpredictable things, it would be to try my craft at ground-breaking: in the immensity of Americana.

Hanoi Hanna, Radio Star
(in *The Chelsea Girls*)

My first romance with a prototypical Dragon Lady was with she of just that generic name in the Sunday comic Terry and the Pirates. As important, as a child I was addicted to its dinner-time, fifteen-minute-serial radio adaptation, with its opening clarion gong and temple bell chiming over the chaotic crush and cries of an indelibly imagined "teeming Orient." I say as important, because it forged for me a lasting link between Far East females and the radio. In addition, I was very aware of that honey-tongued orator, alluring Soong Mei-ling, Mme. Chiang Kai-shek, and kind of in love with her, or about as much as any tiny Yankee boy of the time could be. I also was conscious of, and quite pleasantly seduced by, Nippon radio's immortal propagandist, Tokyo Rose. This is to say nothing of Tinseltown's sensual recreations of the real, far-off phenomenon through Linda Darnell as Tuptim and Gale Sondergaard as No. 1 Wife in *Anna and the King of Siam*; and Gale again as the satisfaction-seeking, silent Chinese in Warner's acted-to-a-turn puzzler, *The Letter.*

The Dragon Lady has choice hanging space in my writer's rogues' gallery of foreign women, all of whom must always be mysterious, dangerous, beautiful, smoldering, fiery—and articulate in an accent to die for. As with Tondalayo, they are emblems of Escape. By the time I was six years old, I had a fully developed objective correlative in the Exotic Brunette, and a Coney Island sense of exactly what I wanted her to be.

The serious architectonics of that Coney Island caricature seized center stage for the first time (in the filmwork) in my string of little political plays whirled around a fascinating female, because they are cast as, but are not, parodies. That artifice begins, of course, with *The Life of Juanita Castro*. I was so taken for a spin by *Juanita Castro*'s distillery, and immediate acceptance, that I was determined to prove it intentionally seminal to a genre. For there were times when I entertained myself as a completed biography, with certain notions of its periods, categories for its work, and proprieties for the succession of its interest. *Indira Gandhi's Daring Device* is arbitrated to the form, but I'm not certain if it or *Hanoi Hanna, Radio Star* is precedent when I turned the hot spot on other promising, sun-toned seductresses. (I.e., as politicians, they pro forma are seen as utilizing their feminine wiles for political gain, whether this was true [as with Mme. Chiang] or not: for when not, it could be wildly funny.)

As our "police action" in Southeast Asia heated up, Andy exclaimed to me, I remember, turning off the lights and grabbing his brown, peeling motorcycle jacket so we could rush off to a party, "Gee, everybody's doing something about the war, Ronnie, shouldn't we do something about the war?"

When he said it, he was gingerly sidestepping a Jackie-in-Mourning stretched for further aerosoling on the floor, and virtually posing by rolls of his Elsie look-alike Cow Wallpaper hanging from hooks because they needed more contemplation. Both images would figure in pieces I'd do in the seventies: Jackie in the longest and best entry in the political genre, and the cows in a (to be sure) radio-drama recalling Elsie's era, *My Foetus Lived on Amboy Street*. But the cows got immediate mention in *Hanoi Hanna,* and *Hanoi Hanna* was what then demanded immediate attention.

Vietnam, at the time, was a kaleidoscope of Dragon Ladies: Hanoi Hanna, Saigon Sally, and Mme. Ngo Ding Nhu; plus the Tiger Lady and a cornucopia acram with legendary Montagnard guerrilla girls. Since Hanoi Hanna had ready-made historical metaphor in the broadcasts of Tokyo Rose, and was far better known than her Saigon counterpart, and was the embodiment of the mystery of her own voice more than anyone else of the days—her apple of Eve to me as my voice was to Andy—Hanna was an obvious grab-her-and-run-with-it.

The real Hanoi Hanna is Trinh Thi Ngo, a woman presently in her late sixties, whose airway-nom meant Autumn Fragrance. She is slender, fine-boned, and very soft-spoken. She spun countercultural rock and propagandized in a cross of sirenic persuasion and deep, motherly concern. The echo of her haunting, beautiful voice is so strong that veterans returning today to Nam often request the privilege of an audience with her.

The movie *Hanoi Hanna, Radio Star* was tailored for Edie, whose voice was also enchanting, and so possibly written when a title page affixed to the script in 1971 claims it was: in 1965—if after *Indira Gandhi's Daring Device,* then fairly late in the fall. Some researchers insist it was done while *Vinyl* was still fresh in my ear, because Victor's dialogue is so clearly Gerard talking, his tones and patterns, and Scum equally clearly Ondine in his clipped expression, verbal mannerisms, and stuttered short-stops. The script was, in fact, originally titled *Vinyl.* I conceived it as the second loop in a purling of eight, all to be called *Vinyl* because, however individual or apparently contained, they were merely the varied fallout of a single threat. As for that length, periodically Andy talked about doing very long films—four hours long, four days long. *Hanoi Hanna* was shot in the summer of 1966. If it was written more than a year before, that delay can be explained by our being disinclined to do any further filming of my screenplays with Edie after July of '65. Confusing the issue, however, is that *Hanoi Hanna* is indicated specifically for a roving camera—for the films, then, that Andy ordered me on definitely after July.

But I'd have seen the first *Vinyl* in numerous reruns, and the style of this script poses some problems for any '65 date. Like some other later ones, it has a developed sense of The Ridiculous, with a deliberated Abbott and Costello-like dialectic, often attenuated for a purpose to intentional excess, and in paced, repeated patterns. It is also the first instance of performer-placement dialogue, which was to figure throughout the full-cast scenes in *Gorilla Queen*, written in June 1966. That is, a sustained visual approach to dramatic assembly, where the lines make no sense unless they come from the exact position in which I am locating the actors. Given most readers can't hold those locations in their visual memory, it often is necessary to put the piece on its feet even for a first reading to find how, and where, it functions. This is why some commercial directors, trained to think plays are short stories, claim mine read like a nightmare.

And finally, having trouble accepting the loss of his biggest star, Andy had asked me to resume writing for Edie once the Harvard Group had abandoned her, in the spring of 1966.

S ome details:
    —*Hanoi Hanna, Radio Star* is riddled with the breath lengths and melodramatic drop-stops of the man who began his nightly broadcasts with: "Good evening Mr. and Mrs. America and all the ships at sea!" Gabriel Heater was a riveting AM commentator on the day's dreary reality

during an earlier and larger war, and my dad used to listen to him religiously. That somber and negative observer being a mainstay of radio's jubilee days, and his regretful lower register in English being still as much of the language as any permanence in it is for me, I let him establish her rhythm and dictate the flavor of Hanna's diatribes.

—"Her kisses were for Joey ... but her heart belonged to Benny" was the lobby-card copy of *A Medal for Benny*, a completely forgotten World War II soaper that arguably is Dorothy Lamour's best film. New Orleans-born Dorothea De Flores, as poseur at least, was another tropical siren in my beckoning gallery-full. Jack Smith said, "She never cut a scene she didn't make interesting."

—"News every hour on the hour, bulletins at one," some will agree, is funny because that's exactly what it too often sounds like: the broadcaster not being big on final consonants.

—Wistaria: i.e., so we hear "star," something these characters and those in the next script want you to know.

—The Parrot Stand was a fixture in Andy's studio, a tall pole with a hoop soldered to the top. Billy Linich used it, among other things, to secure mikes and hang troublesome wires. It figures in a number of famous photos, sometimes with a shaving mirror fixed into the hoop. This stand being always visible to me when I stared into space at the Factory, it was inevitable that I would live with an afterimage of it and involuntarily align it with the Parrot's Beak in Nam— referred to daily on newscasts of the war. It took center stage as a torture rack when I developed *Hanna* into a play for Edward Albee's Playwrights Unit in 1970. (In that form it is called *Vinyl Visits an FM Station*, and is easily my most complex one-acter.)

—If others were present, the phonograph played

continuously at the Factory, and I heard no song more exhaustively than "I Can't Get No Satisfaction." I was particularly fond of this cut and as much would have assumed *Voice* critic Robert Pasolli when he claimed, not disapprovingly, that the sole subject of all my work is frustration. *Hanna* pays tribute to that frequent accompaniment to my thoughts on Forty-Seventh Street, as well as to "I'm Just a Pretty Boy" and other favorites up there.

—A text in an undergraduate course that I took was a Modern Library Giant called *The Wisdom of India and China.* Every time I glanced at the titular audacity of that single volume, I compulsively thought, "Sounds like a bargain." In the scenario, it becomes an uncharacteristically bitter slur of righteous indignation re the capsule-comment mentality of time-conscious America's involvement in Asia.

The Chelsea Girls is a somewhat arbitrary cobbling together of twelve thirty-five minute reels completed in the summer of 1966, placed side by side for the most part, using two projectors, so that they run to approximately three and three-quarters hours. Some of them actually were shot in the old Chelsea Hotel on West Twenty-Third Street. At the time, it was a reasonably priced, semi-dilapidated landmark, a favorite with druggies, alkies, artists, writers, and rock people.

I had no hand in directing the scripts of mine that were used in *The Chelsea Girls,* and the conventional wisdom on this is that I was so miffed at the Emily Brontë transfer that I washed my hands of further helming chores chez Andy. But the truth is, I was on the coast when the epic was lensed. Billy Linich, who had some feel for my work, guided the better part of both *Their Town* and *Hanoi Hanna,* as is obvious from the heavy responsibility assigned to their complex

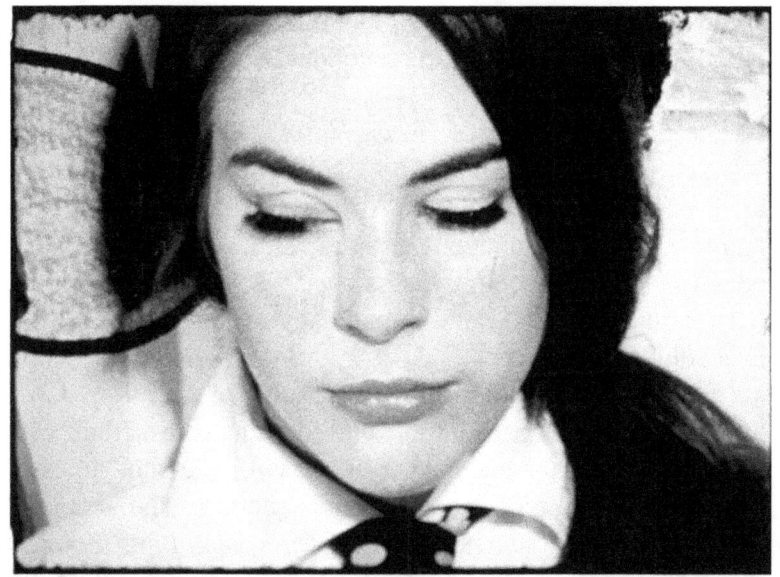

Mary Woronov in Andy Warhol: "The Chelsea Girls" (1966)

lighting, though he modestly claims now to have been only one of a team that saw them through. Since *Hanoi Hanna* promulgates *Vinyl*'s overall simile of sadomasochism, Mary Woronov, in her guise of dominatrix, was a shoo-in for the title role and acquits herself professionally. Edie's "health" absented her from the onerousness. Though aristocratic Susan Bottomly as Victor and Ms. I. Superstar as Scum appear to have little familiarity with the script, Mary and Pepper Davis as G.I. Joe (a stringy blonde chosen for her passive, put-upon look) struggle to make some sense of things without them. Film students often take Mary for a very convincing drag, but I find her no more epicene as Hanna than Hollywood's hard-boiled female legends from Davis and Crawford to Turner, Stanwyck, Russell, and Reynolds; amidst a deal of stiff personality competition in this famous "mirror of the sixties"—Eric Emerson, Brigid Polk, Ondine, Mario, and Nico—Mary emerges a top contender.

The political vision of *Hanoi Hanna, Radio Star* is more detailed than that in *The Life of Juanita Castro*: not different, but more specific (America's romance with war) and more compassionate. It also develops an ungiving, hard-edged border for the political science pieces. Sentimentality, here as in every protoconditional analysis that was to follow, is absolute anathema.

I intended the remaining six sections in the larger *Vinyl* all to be set in this S-M garage and to all feature as their cast these same half-dozen gang members, with one-shot "guests" who might lend their name to their section. The sections' single-sentences pitches (in *Outline for Remaining Spirals*) imply that they all will be political in argument, with fully four again relating to Asia. Unfortunately, other projects, especially theatrical ones, intervened or took priority, and once sufficient time had passed, I lost them.

But whenever I have occasion to deal in particular with *Vinyl Visits an FM Station*, I think, "Oh-me-God! some day I've got to get around to ..."

In partial recompense for this capital gain tax when I transferred to live theatre activity, Ismail Merchant, the producer behind Merchant-Ivory Films, thought he'd make capital of *Indira Gandhi's Daring Device*'s screaming headlines on the subcontinent, and commissioned me to a lengthy treatment concerning no less than five ambitious, affairs-of-state females: to be called when produced, *Jamalistan*. I loved the cash, Ismail loved the treatment, but Ivory didn't see what the fuss or seriousness was all about. And Ivory is nothing if not serious. End of *Jamalistan*.

Their Town
(in *The Chelsea Girls*)

A ndy was concerned about an article in *Life* (March 4, 1966) called "The Pied Piper of Tucson" that dealt with a short (5'1") and strange young lover named Charles Schmid who'd killed a number of teenage girls over a period of years and buried them in the desert. His attention was nailed from the start with the fact that "the townspeople," as he put it, "knew about the murders and never said anything—including the mothers of the girls!"

Before letting me see it, Andy primed me for this oddity's profile with his excited emphasis, a mixture of the mesmerism in the bizarre and his consignment to violent eschatology. And I must say that I myself was taken even before reading it by the prospect of a town that turned the other way.

The importance that Andy attached to this project is evident in its premeditation, its being the most elaborately produced of his films. No other was tried out so many times or with so many different approaches. There were plans for rear projections of its murder sequences as silent flashbacks, to accompany a static presence of heavy dialogue. It would be easy to think that the dumb-show footage is yet another attempt to skirt the opposition of performers not serious or intelligent enough to learn lines, but some of these rolls have sound. Sound or silent, they were a cinematic idea that I trace to Gerard from the start. Though apparently never realized—

i.e., no reels of *Their Town* shot against rear projections have as yet been uncovered—the shorter, unreleased rolls that do survive show the effort that was made to get this tale of eerie mayhem right. Mary, among others, incidentally, appears in a few of the prospective backdrops, but not in the eventually selected, dialogued feature. The work's originality stems in great part from Billy Name's gelling, shrewdly, multiply reflected in the glass-chipped disco ball, a street-found object that was a fixture at the Factory, and that he rotated on the floor for the shootings.

My own subconscious familiarity with the material surfaces in the seeming choicelessness with which I almost immediately eased into the visual and symbolic representation of a town, and an America, that turned its back on the repeated dispensation of death. Most likely written in late March and early April of 1966 (or possibly in mid-May), *Their Town* took me two full weeks to complete, the longest I'd ever spent on a Warhol screenplay. That was not because the weight of gory details sandbagged its progress with impasses so much as nightmares. The ghosts of the slain girls haunted my restless sleep, and the sleeplessness made it difficult to stay chained to my desk long enough to get much done the next day. I also became thoroughly paranoid, and worried about how the accused would receive news of what I was doing. During the developing of *Their Town* into a rock-music drama for the American Place Theatre in 1968-69, I communicated with Schmid, and though he did not object to my writing about him (as you might predict from his cries for attention in the script), he did threaten to fly the pen via levitation should I not do justice by him, and "get" me. He was passing his time in unfamiliar isolation by carving leather miniatures which he offered as gifts to those still willing to pay him mind, among them a perfect and very elaborate show saddle.

In addition, and rather unnervingly, he wrote short stories himself, largely megalomaniacal fantasies in which he fell asleep in caves, and schemed of killing girls—both in the caves and out. He asked if I wouldn't rewrite them for him, making any improvements I saw fit, particularly in the schemes. I drew blanks.

The visual authority that crisscrosses theme and problem in *Their Town* required a matching verbal equivalent. That is found in how the characters often do not seem to hear each other, or hear a pun instead and so pick up on a group-linking but alternate meaning. I belonged to a choral speaking club when I was in junior high, and I thought of the cast's rhythmic ensemble work here as choral speaking. Hence, but for the film's theme as well, it's rhyme that they hear rather than the word itself, as in "people" being heard as "steeple."

As for who really directed this movie while I was in California, Billy says, as of *Hanoi Hanna*, "We all did!": meaning the actors along with the Velvet Underground and Williams, Morrissey, Malanga, Andy, etc. But Billy's lighting and sensitivity in drawing out Eric Emerson's touching, humane performance is what dominates this film. Pepper, Susan Bottomly (screen-named International Velvet), and a large cast all fall into adequate line, but Ingrid makes a pain of herself throughout, affecting gross boredom which she might have evaded by living in Tucson.

The Velvet Underground's score recommends itself for its intense beauty. The film's technicolor outcome, a kind of light-show in itself, would lead Andy into a new eschatological series: of color skulls and the like, placing *Their Town*, so far as it is a Warhol work, squarely in his death and violence genre.

The story editor at Paramount, Michael Silverblatt, KCRW-FM's "Bookworm," and other of the interested identify *Boy on the Straight-Back Chair*, the stage version of *Their Town*, as the work that launched the serial-killer genre. So its importance to me as a pronouncement on mythic America, death and America, and Americana in general, is incalculable; and as Andy's imprint on me beyond The Ridiculous, his extensive legacy.

Their Town was released as a feature, but subsequently incorporated into *The Chelsea Girls*.

S ome details:
——The "Never Marry a Blonde" song: I grew up near Coney Island where, as a kid, I was fascinated with a burlesque queen named Tirza, a classy and willowy, statuesque blonde who showered in wine. She sang a song that began with a semblance to this admonition and went on to elaborate in ways now lost to me. That "mother" appears to Toby much as Tirza did to me over the years, and as other, half-forgotten figures that filled my dreams while writing *Their Town*.

——How forthright the absence of fathers and murdering of only teenage girls: facets of a mother-problem first explored in *The Life of Lady Godiva*, written approximately seven months before this screenplay, and partially felt, partially reflected on as an adjustment to Thornton Wilder's criminal action in writing *Our Town*.

Movie Talk
for Mary Woronov

My stage play *The Life of Lady Godiva* opened at the Play-House of The Ridiculous on April 21, 1966, and ran until it was busted on May 15th and taken to court as a case engagingly coded "The City of New York vs. *The Life of Lady Godiva*." The City won, fined the *Lady* for disrobing without a C. of O., and closed the theatre. I normally didn't write during a New York run in deference to its nearly daily problems, prima donna traumas, and assorted technical emergencies. And on this show, on some nights I even cranked the ancient dimmer board we used on West Seventeenth, and was present when a gelled spot overheated, exploded, and ignited Godiva's wig. Since the fire was doused on stage, the audience assumed the spectacle was intentional, and someone in a back seat enthused vociferously, "Gee! What a great effect!"

In June we moved to a loft at 332 The Bowery and Bond, and under its skylight I wrote *Gorilla Queen*. I took off for the Coast around Independence Day.

In the fall, after *The Chelsea Girls* had been successfully premiered, Andy wondered what my next project should be. We concluded, regretfully, that since Mary Woronov was the only performer he had then willing to learn lines, mightn't I reward her with a feature-length monologue? and we'd do a movie in which she appeared solo. At the time, she was basking in his full favor, though that was not to last long. The fact that her monologue is called "Mary Woronov" as opposed to "Mary Might"—which he himself had dubbed her—shows that considerable tension between them already existed, and that she wanted out from the domination of his removing her—in her own word—"identity," the better to make her his property—something new and aggressive that was gaining unbecoming momentum at the Factory that fall.

Conceding to her talent, the monologue does not entirely express Mary in her own voice or speech patterns, as do roles for Edie, Ondine, Roger, and Gerard. That is, this rumination gives her some leeway to find herself as another. The "superior" in it by whom she is troubled is more a cross of Vaccaro and Warhol than simply Warhol, and the subject matter reflects her own reality right then only in part, though it is there throughout in the hostility and especially the ringing phone which she won't pick up on: as I'd been with her when that happened on a number of occasions. The shadowy, wordless character she appears to address half-heartedly, an enigmatic listener or watcher, is an inevitable emanation given the direction in which the scenarios were moving, or so it seems to me, and an effect I already was incorporating into the Off-Broadway plays (e.g., some stage versions of *Screen Test* in particular).

By the time I came up with her monologue, there was open warfare between Mary and Andy: Andy put the script on hold, Mary's mother sued him for back payments, won $1,000, Mary left the Factory definitively, and *Movie Talk for Mary Woronov* went into the rapidly expanding dustbin of indie history.

Early the following year, I called her for the female lead in the Play-House of The Ridiculous's premiere of *Kitchenette* (an expansion and staging of *Kitchen*), and she acquitted herself with honors—and a faithful theatre following. At Easter time, *Gorilla Queen* premiered at the Judson Memorial Church, and I later wrote the epic *Arenas of Lutetia* for her, which played the Judson in 1968. She subsequently appeared in revivals of *Kitchenette* as well as a revival of *Vinyl Visits an FM Station* in 1972.

Mary went on to a screen career in Europe and Hollywood, and though she is best known for *The Chelsea Girls, Rock 'n Roll High School, Parts I and II*, and *Eating Raoul*, she truly has appeared in more films than you could comfortably see in a month of non-stop screening. Today she's known as a representational painter and short fiction writer as well as an actress.

Jane Eyre Bare

J*ane Eyre Bare* is my final screenplay for Andy Warhol Films, Inc. Appropriately, it is the fullest, the longest of them, the most commercial, the most sustained in comic effect and linear in fidelity to its narrative. But it was written in an atmosphere that was defined for me by desolation and violence.

My sense of the Factory when I returned from the Coast is caught in that filtered heat of the late summer, late afternoon sun falling through its streetside windows, and on Danny Williams at his desk, increasingly bizarre in appearance, his hair matted, his glasses broken, encounter by encounter progressively lost to amphetamine. We have poets who've said that that close-to-setting slant of afternoon sun is their favorite amongst dwindling moments, but it was always the still and most silent part of the day that I liked least, a sickly yellow dotted by the peculiar disappearance of aimlessly drifting gnats. I would sit next to Danny at his massive desk and watch him scoop out the grime from its chisel-work with a penny. How many speed-freaks have I stared at in wonder doing that! But the others, like Ondine, chatted non-stop in accompaniment to their housekeeping. His nose always running, Danny sniffled a bit, but was otherwise very quiet.

At times we were alone, sometimes Andy was there, air-brushing at a distance, or fussing with stretching frames, crouching, his back to us.

And then one day Danny was gone. On September 5th I took a call at the Factory from his mother, asking anxiously if we had seen her son or knew of his whereabouts. "Andy," I relayed, "she wants to talk to you. She's very worried."

"Oh," he groaned, "what a pain. He's a pain, now she is. Tell her I'm not here."

"She knows you're here: I just said I'll get you."

He didn't respond. He knit his brows and turned away from me, and kept working. After I hung up on Mrs. Williams, by way of admonishing me, he concluded dismissively, "I don't care where he is. He's just an amphetamine addict."

Three days later, Gerard told me that he'd learned they found his car by the water, he wasn't sure where, a river in Connecticut or the ocean off Cape Cod, with all his clothes piled neatly beside it. Danny had drowned himself.

I felt too uncomfortable now to pace my off days at the Factory, flipping through the papers and fashion zeens, or listening to the new crowd, looking like they should not have been let off the pages of *Gentlemen's Quarterly*, spin their wheels, the Factory being but one hopeful pit stop on their rounds of the city in search of a fame and fortune that had no strings (like work) attached to it. When Andy was there alone it was worse. He returned to drawing, but almost precise duplicates of his floating, little girl and boy cutouts: which he still on uneasy occasion cashed in on as an illustrator for I. Miller Shoes. Sometimes the childish figures seemed to dangle from a clothesline or a rope necklace. He did that when he was tense and it made me tense.

I busied myself writing a new stage play, a romantic, large-cast, fantasy tragedy called *Atlantis*. It is a three-act epic that almost no one knows about because I considered it a failure. I've completed other plays since that I feel do not work, but none was ever so long, so lyrical, so detailed or elaborately brocaded.

Then early one autumn morning Andy called me: "Oh

Ronnie, come up, there's lots of fairies here!" he enticed facetiously. He was in unusually fine fettle when I got there, he'd been negotiating with Huntington Hartford III to produce a commercial feature. It was to be lensed exotically, out on Bimini where Huntington had an estate.

He told me he'd like a screenplay based on Charlotte Brontë's oft-recycled *Jane Eyre* and, oddly, as a vehicle for Edie. Oddly, because though she'd pop up at the Factory from time to generously spaced time, she was long past her days as a Warhol "star" so to speak, as well as the health needed to undertake so much work. But the producers judged her press bankable and so the opening spirals make clear that the script is constructed around leotarded Edie. While I was at work on the project, it became evident to Andy beyond dispute that Edie would not pan out, and while Andy debated over whether or not Baby Jane Holzer should play the female lead, it is interesting to note that the text begins to veer steadily away from the middle lane in which it held the Jane Eyre character and build up Bertha in the basement and several other hitherto background figures. For although I switched my working title to *Baby Jane Eyre*— which, frankly, I disliked—Baby Jane herself wavered back and forth over this deal when it was proposed to her, and in the end, I had no mental image of Jane Eyre posing before me while I punished the typewriter with my heavy touch because I'd no idea whatsoever of who would play her.

The same obtains for the male lead Rochester, since despite, or rather because of, its Jack-Benny's-butler political incorrectness, I had in mind that an African-American should undertake the role, and couldn't be sure the producers would bite. Rufus Collins was the only black male that Andy previously had starred (in or on the notorious *Couch*), but he wandered greener pastures by then. (Andy had had a black lover some years before I met him. He turned up one night as the drink dispenser at a party we attended: Andy, recognizing him, went beet red, and the Drella Dellas were abuzz for days. Is it any wonder, making the Benny and cocktail party connection, that I just had to have at Andy in an adaptation of his (girlishly) favorite novel?)

Writing without specific leads was not my biggest problem, though, for my liaison on the project was Fu Fu Smith, which whom I'd progress-confer at breakfast time. Hating American breakfasts, he'd order chicken-in-the-basket at seven a.m. and sometimes wasn't sober then. On one such occasion, when we returned to Andy awaiting us at the Factory, he removed a revolver hidden about his person and took some pop-shots at the ceiling. Fu Fu liked me a lot, finding me "different from the others on Forty-Seventh Street," and I, well, certainly found him different, and we got along quite well; but, somehow, I'd felt safer when I traveled alone in Western Sahara.

In November the nerve-shattering Sammy the Italian incident occurred, in which a spaced-out friend of Ondine's took a gun to Andy's head and began to play Russian Roulette. If equally melodramatic, it seemed to me one could live longer on the theatre scene: and I as well was enjoying my longest run there at the time, a double bill of a composite of my (by then) four different *Screen Test* scripts, called simply *Screen Test*, plus *Indira Gandhi's Daring Device*.

Though I was fêted by the Hartford people and received small advances from them for *Jane Eyre Bare*, due to their unresolved struggle over entitlements with Andy, it was evident by March or April of 1967 that the project had fallen through.

That *Jane Eyre Bare* was to have been realized on Bimini explains the inflation of the West Indian locale, merely recalled in the novel. But the script seizes on the majority of its opportunities in that setting, from scoring the perhaps wishful thinking behind a black Rochester and a colonial tension that reflects on the Indochina war to diluting the threat of, and harnessing the violence I perceived in, working at the Factory. Typically, Mutt and Jeff (from the well-loved comic strip of my childhood) are drafted for the Big and Little Savage routines, which cloak and deepen the anger awoken by western Christian expansionism. A wistful and effetely distanced decay is obliquely referenced by incorporating Andy's floating silver pillows (first exhibited at the Castelli Gallery in April 1966). The piece as a whole appears to talk up our having to come to survival terms with ambiguity and, fittingly, sums up the ethical ambiguity of the Warhol world—of people like Edie and Ondine, Philip, Gerard, and Roger and Tosh, and, most of all, Andy himself. But, equally fitting, its general gesture is my evolved decision that it must not in itself "say" the film. So its themes of repression, punishment, and wasted lives in a catchall of ambiguous morality are "literary" themes, as, again, those of *Horse*, while this screenplay like a decorated vessel waits for the film to fill it up.

Jail

There is an old jailhouse on the corner of Second Avenue and Second Street, said to have been a nightly lockup in its last years of service, but which was standing vacant and boarded up for as long back as I can remember. Jonas Mekas, the somewhat shady journalistic promoter of underground indies and founder of the Filmmakers' Cinematheque, prevailed upon the city to turn it into a sound studio, film archive, and new headquarters for his Cinematheque. Jonas let moviemakers he favored use its facilities gratis for editing and/or lensing, and in the summer of 1967, though it struck me as bringing coals to Newcastle or dolts to L.A., Andy was availing himself of the still-intact cell blocks to shoot an improvised color feature called, in the clipped Warholian tradition, *Jail*.

I was making an appearance there on some business and discovered him almost buried in a bevy of chic male coattail-hangers, cover boys lost somewhere between *Vanity Fair* and *Better Body Power*. In a situation reminiscent of *Bitch*, the improv was faltering, and he asked me to step in and move it along. I was not very much in the mood, seeing myself at the moment as a wryly distant dignitary revisiting the scene of his 'umble origin, but did some through-the-bars dialoguing to the boys in the cell adjoining the one I was filmed in.

The occasion stays with me less for the day's dubious recorded theatrics than for the strange and compromising liberty that a tall, strapping fellow, resembling a farmhand, took in manhandling Andy. They may or may not have been sharing a brief, socially miscegenatious affair, but I found having to stand next to these roughhouse intimacies downright embarrassing.

I sometimes visited Andy's spanking new, high-tech office down on Union Square in 1968, but things were just not the same. "Factory" seemed to the then current entourage too corny a collar for the premises; now it would be a very plain "Studio." And the entourage were office workers. The great and wild filmmaking people of his lensing heyday were gone, and after he was shot by Valerie Solanas on June 3rd, with few exceptions an altered Andy retired personally from his cottage industry but bartered away his good name as executive producer to those subsequent "Warhol" efforts so clearly not Warhol. By then I was established as a playwright myself and, omitting *Secrets of the Citizens' Corrections Committee*, which I created for Richard McGuinnes and James Stoller, my own occasional forays into film work were limited to treatments and sketches for daytime TV and mainstream movies.

In recent years, however, I've come back to indie screenwriting, one hopes with some evidence of a lifetime's reflecting on it.

E die Sedgwick, leaving little for the grave, choked on the vomit of her ODing one night in Santa Barbara and died there in November 1971. Marie Menken and Willard Maas, while they were still in their fifties, collapsed after bingeing and died within three days of each other. I lost track of Buddy Wirtschafter, Gregory Battcock, and Aniram Anipso, but in time learned that they too had passed away.

Ingrid Superstar became a bag lady during the eighties, and was picked up by the police half frozen one morning out in Jersey. She was working in an upstate mill in 1988, and leaving her post for an apparent break, her cigarettes and purse in place on her desk, she wandered down to a river beside the workhouse and was never seen again. Years of drug and alcohol abuse had damaged Ondine's liver beyond regeneration, and though he went clean in 1975, he never fully regained his health, strength, or remarkable wit, and died of liver failure in his mother's home out in Queens in 1990.

Eric Emerson brought suit against Andy in the early seventies for non-payment on all the long films in which he'd acted, but Andy's lawyers stalled the trial until Eric went to Italy, then scheduled it and in his absence had the case voided for the plaintiff's failure to appear in court. In May 1975 he either ODd on heroin or was murdered, his body carelessly tossed into the street and his bicycle broken and thrown beside it to simulate a traffic accident. Couldn't have fooled a rookie nark, but there was no investigation.

Following several admittances to Beth Israel on Stuyvesant Park and East Fifteenth, the lifelong semi-celibate Jack Smith startled everyone by revealing that he was suffering from complications related to AIDS, and succumbed there in September 1989.

I brought suit against Andy myself for back payments in 1971, but eventually dropped the litigation when I realized his need to dominate and outdo would sooner see his attorneys bleed him blue to the cleaners than square off with me. Convinced I detested him, he found it hard to swallow his pride, but suggested we do some Hollywood movies together rather than continue disputing. I felt he was dreaming qua usual re Hollywood, but was altogether too emotional by then, in light of what I considered to be his ingratitude, to entertain collaborating any further. In a remarkable gesture of competitiveness, he withdrew from circulation all the films that I'd written and directed myself and secreted them away under lock and key for the remainder of his life—and then some, via his estate.

Around 1980, Professor Bertram attempted to effect a reconciliation between us, more related to my initially modeling for Andy as had been my first standing with him, rather than writing again. He reports that Andy was interested, but I remained inflexible, which I relate knowing how unforgivable that now must sound. In my defense, I believed one's mutualities survive no hiatus.

Andy, of course, went on to become the most famous artist of the century: and, unattended, despite his estimated worth of two-thirds of a billion dollars, after being administered a dose of Cefoxitin following routine gallbladder surgery—Cefoxitin, to which he was allergic—bled to death on February 22, 1987.

There is in snow or rain a conduct as strong as voices. Once in a wood by a stream in Pennsylvania, on a blind and moonless night I stopped by a thick stand of birch and felt I couldn't move. A presence was holding me there. Though I could see no thing or no one, a person I knew then who held my life in his close and unargued jurisdiction, not daring to exhale, was inches away from me.

On a snowy night many years after I gave very much thought anymore to film or the Factory, I was walking north on Park Avenue near where Max's Kansas City had once been. It was late, very cold, and except for myself I thought deserted. Then I stopped because suddenly I felt that I couldn't move. I waited and listened to my own breathing.

Then he called to me. "Hello, Ronnie."

His voice was gentle, and very even. He was standing alone in a doorway. Perhaps he was waiting for someone, or more likely a group of people. But at that moment, on that night, he was alone on a wide and dark, deserted street filling up with snow. The man whose career-long image was that he went nowhere unless in the protected center of a jet-set pack, was leaning quietly against a doorjamb, as alone as he some nights was when I first went to work for him.

With my heart beating rapidly, I took a half-dozen steps to my right so that I came up close to him. I looked down rather than stare hard at his face because this time there would be no instructions in his face for some art that had to be made, and made very soon.

Instead, we stood together in silence for several minutes. Then I went on up the street in the snow.

Appendix:
The Roots of the Theatre of The Ridiculous in the Scripted Films of Andy Warhol

I
Corrections: The Theatre of The Ridiculous, 1965-1996

I had developed those styles which I collectively called "The Ridiculous" in order to center a rage for retaliatory iconoclasm in a series of aggressively deconstructive events. Their construals of frustration or helplessness were suggested for consideration as a source of ethics; and their alarm in waiting—the waiting, for instance, of a child believing her or himself lost in a mega department store—was meant to be read as so neurotically imaged as to effectively cancel it as a legitimacy of cosmic desertion.

The Ridiculous, then, was not to be limited to the demotic dialogues, or to the obsessive and vulgar—the abandon in (perceived) abandonment. But that all under the aegis, as always noted, are autotelic seems the unforced and unavoidable prudence occasioned by their temperamental origin. If fury catoptrically extending nullification and panic into diction itself for the conjuration of characters, with their misheard names inventing their natures, is what is being revised—and The Ridiculous should be experienced as continuous revisal—then its dramatic praxis would appear to warrant those wardens of self-reflexiveness, occasional shattered density, or sudden endings; and a perhaps enduring, but at least immediate, attentive tentativeness.

The name "Ridiculous" came before the publicly produced stage events: even before the screened screenscripts. It was a signifier-in-search-of other signifiers for subjects—was A-Name sailing for ten years toward Ithaca with a satchel of sabbatical brochures for every island on the way.

While in college, while staring at the main quadrangle during a lecture on Theatre of the Absurd, I wondered: "What next?" Meaning, "What in the world could come after a Theatre of the Absurd—Theatre of the Ridiculous??" Which was to say, how far could you push this (bulldozer), how steep the descent (from the Greeks), and is there rock bottom? and who cares?

Then this, a signifier exhausting rackfuls of other signifiers as if to wear out a salesperson in the mischievous id, was to become a conscious process, and I can't exaggerate how mainstay, in the method of The Ridiculous. *Gorilla Queen*[4], for instance and above all, a title suggested to me by my brother taking umbrage at the observation of a mutual acquaintance[5], clearly was a name which eventually would need a play-on-names. To be sure, there is a long if unhonored tradition to the naming of phenomena which do not exist—which naming, on a day still yet to come, summons them. In Filmdom it was SOP for moguls to compile titles they felt guaranteed box for programmers and to assign those, after gross mismanagement, punitive delays, and the insolence of office, along with an irrelevant budget and six-week deadline, to contract directors and their writers. Hence classics like *Curse of*

---

4   By consensus, the quintessential Ridiculous theatre piece. In *The Best of Off-Off-Broadway*, ed. Michael Smith (New York: E.P. Dutton & Co., 1969); *The Off-Off-Broadway Book: The People, Plays, Theatres*, ed. Bruce Mailman & Albert Poland (New York: Bobbs-Merrill Co., 1972); and in foreign-language editions. A musical, *The Nutcracker in the Land of Nuts* (1979), is a later and much simpler, very clear illustration of the same process.

5   A friend of Lanny Powers (a Pop forerunner, installation artist, and the logoist and set designer for *The Life of Lady Godiva*), one Michael Gehring, an unusually large, very full-black-bearded, and generally hairy man, now of San Francisco, invited Harvey Tavel to dinner one evening and afterward complained that he could hear him chewing. When this got back to him, Mr. Tavel, near choked with exasperation, gasped: "Well! I'll be damned if I take etiquette lessons from a—from a—gorilla queen!"

the Cat People, Every Day's a Holiday[6], *The Gang's All Here, If I'm Lucky, Something for the Boys, Devotion, White Savage*, and *Tarzan's Greatest Adventure*[7] which, pointedly enough, struggle to find something in common with their designations.

Fortunately this process, creatively arbitrary, fascinated me: because it was how almost all the Andy Warhol films (Factory-line minus the delays) that I wrote and often directed were to come to be. Because the "now-ness" of the arbitrary challenge, and the tacky glamour of the agenda aside, the sequence had resonance. Wasn't Adam's first act to verbalize into being (viz. "name") the animals in Eden, and wasn't he perpetuating the modus operandi?: And God said, Let there be light, and then there was . . .

Yet one Ridiculous form saw the light of day and dark of official opprobrium eight full years before I realized that there indeed it was: because I didn't take its put/upon put/on put-on seriously— any more than I would all of my screenscripts, or, for that matter, stage events, until 1970 (or so, because by then others presumably were). I had wanted to be a writer: of fiction or poetry. Who amongst one's "sophisticated" peers in those benighted times considered screenwriters writers, or, given "theatre" then, playwrights?[8]

In a "good-old-school-days, rule-days" memoir[9], I've noted the circumstances of the Xmas show I was forced to write by a duplicitous professor and, when it was enthusiastically realized

---

6   Mindless and meaningless title for a Mae West gem.
7   This too vague title has consigned the feature (Paramount, 1959) to action dustbins. Yet one might say it is inappropriately accurate: because, propelled by a dead-serious Gordon Scott in the titular role, the yarn is closer in spirit to Joseph Conrad than Edgar Rice Burroughs. Scott starred in five *Tarzan* entries. All of them are noteworthy, and all go unnoted.
8   The word, of course, does not imply "writer," and its spelling should not be altered to do so.
9   *Brooklyn Literary Review*, Vol. 2 (CUNY-Brooklyn, Fall/Winter 1981-82).

in a classroom situation, the same's vigorous denunciation of it because of his refluent outrage at the way it had come into this world. What he purposefully chose to object to, for in doing so could avoid the satire's core (himself), was its style: which is to say, a Ridiculous one, fully articulated; and which, under the storm of self-righteous protest and harsh punishment that was to follow, was holed up until 1962.

Then this happened:

To take breaks from a novel I was working on[10], I used to meet with friends in the fifth-floor, front-west unit at 27 St. Mark's Place, a three-room railroad I'd previously rented myself but had since turned over to first my brother, and then Ronald Kutny[11]. Conditioned to writing almost daily, I couldn't resist at unsocial moments hitting Ronnie's typewriter to bang out what I then called spirals (episodes unified by theme or completed action) of a Tarzan filmscript. To relieve the strain of the novel's heavy tone, these were always humorous though, emphatically, neither parody nor pastiche. I'd been catching the Weissmuller entries matineed generously on TV; that "underground" films were all the rage in the East Village at the time accounts for the Tarzan-screenscript format: verbose closet-screenscript though it would certainly prove to be. When I'd become tired, someone else, anyone present and willing, really, would sit down and, laughing all the while, continue from where I'd left off. Because it frequently was difficult to pick up a co-author's thread, that spiral structure came in handy. But in the end, the rich, daunting assemblage inevitably

10   *Street of Stairs* (New York: Olympia Press, 1968); as *Stufen* (Darmstadt: Olympia Press Sonderreihe, 1969). The setting is largely Morocco during the last months in the reign of Mohammed V.

11   Lecturer in Linguistics, Mahidol University of Medicine and Science, Bangkok, Thailand, c. 1969 until his death in 1986. A schoolmate, he had a hand as well in the above-mentioned Xmas show. In *Street of Stairs* he is the inspiration for the tale, "RK, the Distraught, the Thrall O' Love" (published as a self-contained piece in *Intransit* (1968), pp. 98-102.

seemed unwieldy and, to be sure, stylistically inconsistent. Although committed to preserving as much of my colleagues' contributions as possible, it seemed wise to redraft it entirely. In addition to a battery of World War II-type antagonists, I narrowed the players down to sixteen Tarzans, twelve Janes, four Boys, and two Cheetahs: with each version of the character boasting its own personality, but these multiple personalities all fairly comfortable playing in scenes with themselves.

Identifying its maniacally referential, self-critical, and autotelic low-culture highbrowism, I called the "junkle" experiment *Tarzan of the Flicks*. And at the insistence of *Flaming Creatures*'s vampire-Harlow, Joel Markman (1935-1994), began enacting it spiral by spiral in 1964 on successive Wednesday night open poetry readings at Café Le Métro (Second Avenue between Ninth and Tenth Streets). Given its audience versed in listening to complex material, and served up after much deadpan poetry, the high jinks were roundly indulged; and I was encouraged to segue this reception with a slew of comic poems, among them the first "movie" ones.[12]

This Ridiculous, and definitively as such it was, *Tarzan of the Flicks* never was filmed, but selections from it were published by Ron Norman in *Blacklist* No. 6. That led to a staging of them in December 1965 at Goddard College, Vermont, with the entire student body (needed) in the cast. David Mamet, then attending Goddard, has told me his role in *Tarzan of the Flicks* constitutes his maiden countercultural theatrical experience. Mamet, then, is the first later-to-be superluminary to have been tarnished by The Ridiculous, and not any number of other people for whom this claim commonly is made in irresponsible accounts.

---

12 See *Wormwood* (April 1965), *Tri-Quarterly* No. 4 (Winter 1965), *Graffiti* No. 2 (1965), *Night*, 1990 (New York: Perich Publications).

The shot scripts predated the live events—another cold fact constantly misstated, particularly by film historians, who with increasing frequency insist that I somehow wrote the scenarios Warhol commissioned before I knew of his existence.

Andrew Warhola came to Café Le Métro in November 1964 to scare up voices for sound film, his next project. According to his right-hand man at the time, poet Gerard Malanga, at Gerard's suggestions, specifically to hear me. Impressed by my fairly stagy delivery and/or voice, Andy asked me to his table and immediately invited me to read onto the track of an Auricon 16 mm sync-sound movie he was set to shoot concerning Jean Harlow (1911-1937), the subject of cinema and top-seller bios that season. "To read really anything," he said, "your poetry, or novel. Or better yet, the telephone directory. I know you'll make it interesting. But try not to."

Geared for that, but mildly stunned by an eleventh-hour Warholian whack, a favorite creative electric-cattlepunch of his, my role in *Harlot*[13], shot on December 13th, was switched to impromptu raconteur, directing and entertainingly parried by Brit poet Harry Fainlight and the artist's Factory photographer, studio manager, and long-time friend Billy Linich (a k a Billy Name). A week later, I sat for my cameo in the two-and-a-half-hour pastiche *Fifty Fantasticks*.

Then, in January 1965 Andy's companion, the unusually prepossessing Philip Fagan, envious and eager to rid the Factory of everyone in the Warhol entourage except myself, with whom alone he felt at ease, advised Andy to take me on as script-writer—of vehicles for himself solo, Andy to direct. Capitulating to Philip's whim, Andy ordered my first formal scenario, *Screen Test* (in filmographies, *Screen Test #1* or *Philip's Screen Test*).

---

13   *Andy Warhol: Film Factory*, ed. Michael O'Pray (Indiana University Press, 1990), *Film Culture* No. 40 (Spring 1966), etc. Scenario and various lengthy commentaries on the film.

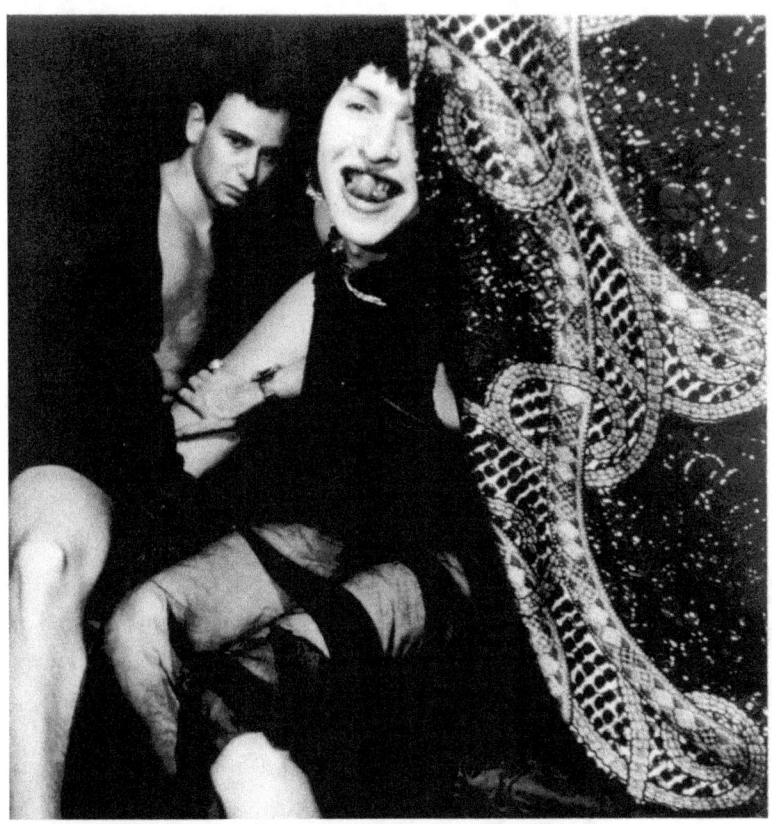

Ronald Tavel (left) and Joel Markman, 1963. Photograph by Jack Smith.

I conducted the unedited audition o.c., directly facing Philip, who, to our astonishment, despite apparently getting his way, physically internalized, staring deeply at me and the relentless, grinding Auricon; and the seventy-minute still-held close of him, increasingly iron-jawed, finished with equal parts insights and enigma. This celluloid record may be read in several ways today, particularly as pertains to the distancing in the artist's exploration of his significant-other relationship, and me, using me as a microscopied distancer. But however he interpreted his findings, it seemed not what he wanted at that point made public.

"We'll do another screen test movie," Warhol concluded, "and, Ronnie, this time use Mario[14]—he should be good." That second try earned his *Good Housekeeping* seal, and so was followed by an average two scripted flickers a month, as suits a factory-image.[15] And Philip was given his walking papers.

Since the screenplays I wrote through to that summer used an unmoving camera,[16] prima facie their format would make them easy to convert into (one-act) stage experiences. During the spring a number of scripts were designed to show off the Factory's then reigning superstar, the huge-eyed girl-who-went-for-it, Edie Sedgwick. But when I appeared with copies of *Shower* (Andy was intrigued with the sexiness of TV shower-soap ads), Edie's self-promoting "friends" and "advisors," whose invisible means of support evidently was her inheritance, bamboozled her into passing on the option in favor of waiting for one amongst them to come up with "something" for her. Andy quickly judged *Shower* to be my best script[17] and, eager not to see it wasted, urged me to have it staged. His connections eventually led to an actor, John Vaccaro—who, after power-brokering through some vividly theatrical and near-violent objections—rushed it into production with *The Life of*

---

14   René Rivera, s.n. Mario Montez, a transvestite counterculture star who took the name of his ideal, Universal's legendary "Queen of Technicolor," Dominican-born beauty Maria Montez (June 6, 1912-Sept. 7, 1951).

15   The shot feature films I scripted for Warhol after January 1965: *Screen Test II, Suicide, The Life of Juanita Castro, Bitch* (in part), *Horse, Vinyl, Kitchen, Space, Hedy, Withering Sights, Hanoi Hanna, Radio Star, Their Town*, and *Jail* (in part). *Hanoi Hanna* and *Their Town* subsequently incorporated into the epic *The Chelsea Girls*.

16   By way of justification for the repeated technique, Warhol had explained to me, "Since that's my contribution (to filmmaking) …" He had carefully studied Edison's 19th C. footage.

17   Published as a one-act play in *The Young American Writers*, ed. Richard Kostelanetz (New York: Funk & Wagnalls, 1967).

Juanita Castro as a curtainer.[18] As a director Vaccaro developed a noisy, dynamic, declamatory style which, referring to Exaggeration Art, is called, exigently, Camp, that would ensure the double bill's reception—though as aesthete Jack Smith claimed, always at the price of their "elegance" and, later, as critic Michael T. Smith would note, sometimes their themes, thrust, intention, and audibility. Be that as it may, this frenetic and flamboyant performance style, which tended to neglect the text, would long remain identified with my Ridiculous works—and indeed all plays whose authors labeled them "Ridiculous."[19] Pointedly enough, it wasn't until Harvey Tavel directed *Kitchenette* (early 1967) in a diagramatically more comprehensible manner, that The Play-House of The Ridiculous won its first awards. Plus, that piece as a result saw immediate publication in *Partisan Review*, then the nation's most prestigious literary and political quarterly.

I have testified[20] that Warhol's entrepreneurial skill is not least apparent in his appreciation of my as then untapped loathing of New York and all things megamodern: which he insisted I express for my growth as a writer even as he sought to exploit that very expression. And he wanted that expression in the most harsh abstract and classical terms. Later, he instructed, you on your own can live with and out your neo-romantic, exotic, and narrative biases. In the stress placed on the late artist's social climbing, star-

---

18   Published as a one-act play in *Tri-Quarterly* No. 6 (1966).

19   Vaccaro went on to stage pieces by Charles Ludlam, Kenneth Bernard, Tom Murrin, William M. Hoffman, Leslie Lee, Bernard Roth, and Rosalyn Drexler, among others. Because he helmed them, and always in this same highly identifiable style, they became known, confusingly, as "Ridiculous" plays. Their authors, evidently finding no wrong in coattail careerism, fell quietly in line.

20   Victor Bockris, *Warhol: The Biography* (London, Sydney, Auckland, Johannesburg: Frederick Muller, 1989). Not to be confused with the inferior American abridgment, *The Life and Death of Andy Warhol,* which reads like a breathless scandal-sniffer.

gazing, strong right-wing leanings, and even calculated cruelties, his stature as a master teacher generally is overlooked (doesn't make good copy).

In mid-July '65, when I actually was about to have that first stage production, I went to visit its program's logoist, the mythic Jack Smith (1932-1989), in whose films and photo-sessions I had worked on occasion since 1962. I checked the logo (four people showering together, now a collector's item) and decided that two unrelated one-acts were a weak draw. Historically, Americans preferred the full-length play, a single experience. The bill needed a catchall to cleverly/wickedly unify it. And "The Theatre of the[21] Ridiculous" leapt immediately to mind. "I shall[22] justify this classifying with a manifesto," I told Smith, "one sentence, so it will fit neatly on the program."

"We have passed beyond the absurd: our position is absolutely preposterous."

Smith liked it. He then asked if I'd ever won any awards, honors, or medals to give the program "authority." Why, yes, in the eighth grade the (ultraconservative) American Legion had pinned me with a History and Civics Medal—for outspokenness, no less. This tweaked Jack's sense of humor, considering the "civic" quidity of our curtain-raiser. He added the honor prominently to the credits, signed his name, and prepared the markup for the printers.[23]

---

21   I originally used lower case for the 't': at the time it only seemed modest. (See below on the pitfalls of sounding superior.) In the interest of clarity, it later was changed by editors.

22   Allen Ginsberg found my use of "shall" in verse transatlantic. So must be my speech.

23   Predictably, mention of the medal would infuriate the p.c. thought police (as do many of my scripts): among them, Stefan Brecht, a self-proclaimed "professional philosopher and communist" who has lived all his life off his father's fat royalties.

Some of my reasoning in the classification was this:

I played for a while with "The Theatre of the Preposterous" as an umbrella. But aside from being clumsy, less arresting, and more pretentious than "Ridiculous," "Preposterous" is too specifically self-limiting to the literal, viz, "putting the behind in front." And while that was flickin' 'em the bird they deserved, I knew how painfully that might someday backfire! "Ridiculous" was Aristotelian and utilitarian. And egalitarian: it avoided the other's Brahman condescension. True, even "The Theatre of the Ridiculous" had too lofty, arch, and somehow smirky a sound to be really safe. But I estimated that while one out of three critics would seize upon it to condemn us,[24] the other two would welcome it as column fodder: and, in doing so, promote us.

My calculation proved accurate for fifteen years. Not the least of the ink waste was an honest effort on four continents to define "The Ridiculous."[25] But the rocky road of The Play-House, milestoned with scandal, occasioned the true attention and pseudo-scholarship: internecine feuds, censorship of college tours, and show shutdowns, as well as courtroom tug o' wars for certificates of occupancy, fire violations, and nudity. Not to forget attitude (read, subject matter), visits by the CIA and FBI, the New York Vice Squad, and a summons to the United Nations its illustrious self.[26]

Today, inexcusably, an illiterate and emasculated Ridiculous

---

24 Reviewer Walter Kerr claimed the classification subsumes criticism: if in any way disparaged, we'd automatically respond, "But of course, it's ridiculous!" Robert Brustein quipped that Kerr held American theatre back by thirty years. Having quipped as much but envious, I assume, Brustein tries his best to outdo him.

25 Peter Michelson, "Pop Goes America," *The New Republic*, Sept. 9, 1967, is one of the best of these.

26 Don McNeill, "Appeal to Washington: Theatre of the Ridiculous Isn't Funny to Indians," *The Village Voice*, March 9, 1967. Also Joseph Lelyveld, "Foreign Minister Warned of Play, etc.," *The New York Times*, March 29, 1967.

Theatre is petted and pampered by the press like the spoiled retard it's become.

Sic transit gloria mundi and mea culpa, since I purposely did not register the label "ridiculous" with City Hall—because, not intending to straitjacket the remainder of my theatrical involvement by writing exclusively Ridiculous pieces, I believed (I am sure rightly) that the classification would be forgotten unless I let others adopt it. That they would adopt only one surface style, rather easy to imitate, and absolutely nothing beneath it is something I never anticipated—and, in the greedy and unconscionable search for ever larger audiences, would dilute even that surface, was clearly not in my unforgivably, and unrescindably, naïve plans.

A painful moment haunts yet which resulted from that sudden shift of invested time from Midtown to East Village. For this tasking with Smith during that spring led to some other joint efforts on his stills and scripts[27] that inevitably would come to Andy's attention. Warhol's controlling powers were phenomenal, almost mystical, and in the end, against all reasonableness except for his fear of desertion, he was able to make me feel guilty. As an act of purification I must relate how in late May of '65, when he caught me at an unguarded moment, he suddenly said, apropos of nothing that preceded it, that he didn't mind my working with Jack Smith. I did not respond, for I was dumbfounded by his temerity.

At the same time, it was impossible not to be moved.

How "The Theatre of the Ridiculous" became "Play-House of The Ridiculous" is so incidental, and so simple, that no account has ever gotten it straight. Once more:

The Life of Juanita Castro and *Shower* premiered on July 29, 1965 at Coda Gallery, an actual art gallery at 89 East Tenth Street,

27   See my essay in *Flaming Creature: The Art and Times of Jack Smith*, ed. Edward Leffingwell (London & New York: Serpent's Tail with The Institute for Contemporary Art, P.S. 1, 1997).

just west of Third Avenue. Since, by Equity ruling, the Coda run was a not-for-profit showcase, SRO from opening night on bought rapid transfer to a commercial situation, the St. Mark's Playhouse on Second Avenue. Shortly thereafter, the Coda ceased to operate, and the historic row nestling No. 89 no longer stands.

Early the next spring, when we were set to go with our followup production, in effect the third work, *The Life of Lady Godiva*, we found a studio with a small proscenium stage over at 13 West Seventeenth Street. Unfortunately, this hall was an outside flight of stairs above the sidewalk, and zoning laws prohibited calling any area more than three steps above the walk a "theatre." So I changed our group's name to Play-House of The Ridiculous, which pun met with majority approval, and we went on.

Technically then, Play-House of The Ridiculous is only a company name. At the movement's zenith there were four separate companies—one a Parisian group calling itself, in English, The Theatre of the Ridiculous. "House" house-director Vaccaro used that company name for the next twenty years, and I, alternating with Theatre of The Ridiculous, have used it all along myself to identify entries I feel so identifiable. For though I split (in effect, but not officially) with Vaccaro's ever new-membered group in early March 1967,[28] I most certainly was not closing my days with

---

28 The break (we've joined forces for only four productions since) followed a dispute between Vaccaro and myself over the use, or misuse, of *Indira Gandhi's Daring Device*, detailed by Mary Grant in "Anti-Indian Obscenity" (*LINK*, a New Delhi newspaper, April 2, 1967) and Ronald Sukenick, *Down and In: Life in the Underground* (New York: Beech Books, William Morrow, 1987). Said dispute led to Vaccaro's rejection of my next offering, *Gorilla Queen*. He claimed it was "pure filth." (!) So typical. Actually, he was covering, having judged that he was incapable of directing it—but suggested, nevertheless, cutting its sixty-eight pages to thirteen. That would have been pure filth. *Gorilla Queen* was then accepted immediately by the Judson Memorial (Northern Baptist) Church, which, declaring it was a study of the Resurrection, got it up elaborately as their Easter '67 presentation(!); sold to commercial interests eight days after opening,

143

that classification or title for such work as I was to and still will write and feel fall inside its definition.[29]

Standard definitions conventionally and most often recently have been confined to its fallout in staunch rejection of a hub: for calling The Ridiculous "metaphysical burlesque" evades/denies that it naturally is, should, or must be ontological as art. Saying that it anarchically undermines political, sexual, psychological, and cultural categories misinstructs its why and how, for in the latter, its dis-closing, it undercategories, which is never anarchic. On the contrary, it calls category an Anarchy of Truth. Saying that it parodies classical literary forms or re-functions American popular entertainments attempts to screen, obviate, or inexplicably exculpate it from the fact that it is classical literary form as popular American entertainment. Calling it *self-conscious camp* carries owls to Athens over camp's only obligation, militant deconstruction. Saying that it is kitsch, grotesque, earthy, primal, liberated, referential to the whole history of American mass

---

it went on to productions across the states, and in Canada, Germany, the Netherlands, Australia, and Asia. Vaccaro went on to cut every script that has come across his desk ever since.

29   One may argue the category of any serious contemporary piece, and perhaps to little profit. Or argue that ideally we should not categorize art works. The Yale Divinity School, taking The Ridiculous as a particular religious outlook, identifies all my theatre writings, including the domestic dramas and formal tragedies, as Ridiculous. But Performing Arts Journal editor Bonnie Marranca divides the later ones into Americana, the heroic or epic, and philosophical melodrama. Whatever the assessments, however, even the narrowest definitions of The Ridiculous (based on the examples of the 1962-67 period) would have to cover such later full-lengths as *How Jacqueline Kennedy Became Queen of Greece* (1973), *My Foetus Lived on Amboy Street* (1976), *The Clown's Tail* (1976), *The Ovens of Anita Orangejuice* (1977), *The Nutcracker in the Land of Nuts* (1979), *Notorious Harik Will Kill the Pope* (1986), *En attendant le tableau...* (1990), and *Estrella Verde* (1992).

culture, flicks and their stars, pop songs, TV, advertising, icons, artifacts, vaudevilles, and musicals—and then saying that it is not intellectual as opposed to The Absurd identifies what nightly theatre attendance does to perception, not The Ridiculous.

I don't wish this to be the thankless task of playing critical historian on vengeful critical historians, or even they who so consciously mislead them. But thirty-one years after the fact, in an international blur of historical fact for which there is now abundant evidence,[30] this is offered as a reminder to those since

---

30   Warhol's biographer, Victor Bockris, claims that a rave notice for *The Life of Juanita Castro* by the then most respected film reviewer in New York (Andrew Sarris, *The Village Voice*, November 11 and December 9, 1965), which placed most of the credit for the work in my corner, instigated Warhol's efforts to conceal me "behind a curtain of silence." On location one day in March 1966, when Dr. Paul Bertram (Dean, Graduate School, Rutgers U.), after perusing the script's "take" on the Brontë novel, asked to speak to the writer of *Withering Sights*, Andy actually physically blocked his view of me and told him he could confer with the feature's lead (a short-on-gray-matter Ingrid Superstar) instead. Jack Smith himself suffered few qualms claiming, on his résumé no less, that he was the "father" of the Theatre of The Ridiculous. "Anything that can help you out," I said (giving it no english) when I spotted that. This tomfoolery can be traced to the misguided and uncharacteristic charity of a befuddled John Vaccaro. Actually, both together should have exhausted anything coherent they had to opine anent Ridiculous theatre in something less than seven seconds. "Historical" works like Robert Heide's recent recollections of the West Village sixties, wildly inaccurate, have added to the confusion. Heide doesn't believe in research, nor for that matter does Bonnie Marranca, whose Introduction to her publication *Theatre of the Ridiculous* (New York: PAJ Publications, 1979, 1983) is a bewildering non-account of the movement boasting more misinformation than one could hope to set straight, which she has never retracted. Not without some charm and humor, KCRW-FM's Bookworm, Michael Silverblatt, recently speculated over the airwaves (The Bookworm, Tavel interview, 1994) on the continuing "disappearance act" of all my stagework, films, and fiction regardless of the number of their presentations, printings, or screenings, and theorized that I participate not a little in this conspiracy. This article, then, toward some rectification.

and still using the designation, of what the Ridiculous, however polysemous, as a mooted Event of Concern, is.

It must reify an ethical weighing anchor, even when its focus is abstracted *in extremis* to deal with nullification—or the absent, the invisible, space, and concave and convex time, as in the film/ stage scripts. It should *momentarily* stabilize a high-rise "con" of constructed binary opposites, and pound away furiously at normalcy and "sanity." It must demythologize western *and* Asian cultural delusion and devastations; it must be religious, political, and educated. And at least as uncertain of itself as it is of others.

Today, Ridiculous companies do "plays." I never intended that. They must offer only *they gathering*, for The Ridiculous is a proposal. It proposes, never supposes theatre.

II
The "Play" as Plenipotentiary

The sense that an artifice is greater than the artificer must signal the successful corporate there of deliberateness and indeterminables. This may be what playwrights misrepresent when they report that their *characters* say what they wish and not what the playwright for preconceived ends would have them, and that they tell their creator what to write. Playwrights also often report that they don't know how a particular work was achieved and that they couldn't, for dear life, repeat it.

The second insight is true because the delicate relationship between their purposefulness and purposes has moved on; but the first is a misunderstanding rooted in their stubborn reading of ourselves as the intentionality of an artwork, and needing to be.

The crafts of stage and screen writing include assembling a field in which one's aware and sleeping being, and textual determinants, may cooperate with minimum static. And this ingenuity can be water on the desert when the time to complete assignments is disturbingly short. Given only four months by Cornell University to come up with a formally complex melodrama (*The Understudy*),[31] I invested two of those in arranging its field by burying myself in accounts of theatre district murders at the newspaper archive on Fortieth Street. The ZBS Foundation gave me one month to write, record, and mix-down the radio play *My Foetus Lived on Amboy Street*,[32] and I devoted the whole first weekend to its field by taking two calculatedly traumatic trips

---

31 *Stiletto* No. 2, ed. Michael Annis (Denver, Colorado: Howling Dog Press, 1992). *Chung Wai Literary Monthly* Vol. 22, No. 9 (Taipei, Taiwan: National Taiwan University Press, February 1994) (in Mandarin).

32 *Brooklyn Literary Review* Vol. 2 (New York: CUNY-Brooklyn, Fall/Winter 1981-82).

right to the patrimonial anxieties of a long-time companion[33] and myself. With the Warhol scenarios, I seldom squeezed in more than seven days between his order for the script and the wrap on that very flick, so that my input on those required experimenting with dependable and, since he forbade repetition, increasingly more resourceful and varied ways to prompt the purpose and repressed of everyone involved into responsiveness.

And along with what I'd already transposed for myself in *Street of Stairs*, and in part because the movie *Horse* openly explored the problem of the mercilessly deadlined script within the context of taking a stab at defining film itself, as relates to this field-finding, our work on *Horse* was to prove paramount in establishing methodology and a world for the Ridiculous event. So I'd like to look a bit at that movie in the making.

In my mid-sixties Manhattan, Beckett, Genet, and Burroughs were revered as one's paradigmatic literary contemporaries. So how I perceived, and naively held was perceived generally, the wannabe writer's task at the juncture at which these three had defined and assigned it to him is something to the point. And that was that commitments to actualize the redemptory or salvational were impassed because (a) those other than the artistic (e.g., religious, medicinal, instructional, political) were often unwilling and uniformly unable to answer the post-Victorian authentification of ourselves as the possibility of possibilities, and (b) potholes in 112 years of epistemological angst had rendered ordinary avenues to any (e.g., the thinking-of-them) obsolete, and (c) we neither could preset nor decal a moral "why" to salvation's availability or advised reality, let alone urgency.

This impasse, then, now had to be celebrated, that is, both objectified and broken up, as opposed to abandoned: since obsolete

---

33 Joanna Schielke, Off-Broadway lighting designer.

avenues do not eradicate a city—or our having to live in it.

Street of Stairs, which required eight months of experiment, was begun formally in 1961 and completed by summer's start in '63. In it, the chronometric tools of historicity and subject are both dismissed and left "recoverable" in nearly forty unidentified apparent-narrators when they confab a rotation in which the asserted, balanced Suspension is then denied via formalities that make a strict necessity of its reassertion (and redenial, etc.).

Horse[34] was shot on the afternoon and evening of April 10, 1965. Andy had selected four good-looking "actors"—poet Dan Cassidy, art critic Gregory Battcock, French-Canadian teenage runaway Larry Latreille, and Hawaiian (funeral) floral designer Tosh Carrillo[35]—and because they suggested cowboys to him, told me he would rent a pony for the shoots. But scripts for film participants to memorize was still two months off. So . . .

While watching the oddly unexpected and sometimes peculiarly slow responses of Charles Boyer and Marlene Dietrich in *The Garden of Allah* (Selznick International, 1936), it occurred to me that those arresting, but glaze-eyed and deliberate, reactions may have been achieved via Richard Boleslawski's not letting either have any idea of what they were going to, and finally did, say next. I imagined this "unexpectedness" was intentional and had been effected by having the filmstars read lines off "idiot sheets" they'd never seen before, and over each other's shoulders; while their intriguing, "searching" adjustments (as if searching for what to say) were the sincere, stylized results of their not having been certain of where exactly off-camera these idiot sheets would next appear.

---

34   *Horse* was restored by the Whitney Museum of American Art in late 1996. It currently is distributed through MoMA.

35   A dazzling counterculture Turhan Bey. Following his '60s artistic and nefarious engagements, he spent ten years teaching/repenting in Central Africa before resurfacing in New York.

Now, my job was to make something we could live with out of four, by fiat, unprepared and thus stage-frightened young men, a pony, an immobile camera, and two thirty-five-minute nonstop reels. I'd need an assistant. If we had four large lacquer cards reading, respectively, "Dan," "Gregory," "Larry," and "Tosh," an idiot sheet for each line of dialogue (two for longer lines, perhaps) and some pure action cards, I figured we'd have a modus operandi at least promising. My idea was to arrange the dialogue sheets in some order that made sense linear or otherwise, and to have Gerard hold these up, consecutively, at a signal from me. I would move along the perimeter of the set (situated by the elevator) with the four name-cards in hand, and choose one appropriate or propitious according to how the shoot was evolving, or what unpredictable turn it had taken; and when I'd flash an actor's name-card, he'd know to look about for, and read or act out whatever dialogue or instruction became visible. Since Andy's factory-time format precluded my own memorizing of the dialogue, I'd have to hold the script in one hand and select the name-cards with the other.[36] This would exact a toll in coordination, concentration, and continuous decisions on the name calls, so I was depending on some real adrenaline under that purposefully manufactured stress. I naturally anticipated that any preset order, no matter what, of the dialogue and action sheets would have to be altered during the shoot, but had libated the assembly-line gods to make this minimal.

Horse's lines implied situation, violence, outlook, and attitudes sponsored by literary themes (the "literature" of movies): which ideally should/would demythologize the West, demythologize

---

36   This convolution is captured in a full-page Billy Name photo in *Andy Warhol: Film Factory*, ibid., ftn. 10. For a photographic tabulation of the shooting of *Horse*, see the chapter on *Horse* in *Stills from the Warhol Films*, photos by Billy Name and text by Debra Miller (Munich-New York: Prestel-Verlag, 1994).

the Western (novel and film), and introduce the hidden in the anthropometric image and stale ethnography of cowboys: their phallic worship and Levi competition, homosexuality, bestiality, onanism, racism, and institutionalized ignorance—and colorful dress and limited vocabulary and diet and facial coding, etc. etc.

Since what people would or would not do when they had nothing to do before a camera had been exploited in the short and feature-length silent portrait or "ageing" films, it became necessary by April to give participants some excuse to be before the camera, some "role," and then to see what would happen. Being distant, stage actors must interpret parts, but the privilege of celluloid was to present us with subjects seven to ten times larger than themselves. The script text then was not conceived of as a discursive text, but rather a pretext (in both senses), because, again, the former belonged properly to fiction, and had to be overridden enroute to discovering film's own identity (a preoccupation at the time). That the red herring text conceivably was interesting in and of itself was only to enrich and closetly complicate the experience: and, actually, to forestall Andy's accusing me of slipping just this side of motion picture neology that April.

What, then, was to be the transaction of this movie?—and how was it to mobilize an identity within Andy Warhol's attention-getting expansion into film, already sensed by some[37] to be inevitable and altogether necessary? Within the polysemy suggested by the Campbell Soup Cans, and even more so by the Brillo Box sculpture, both having their greatest impact by this posture in the filmmaking, seemed couched the 200-year-old dream to remove the artist from the work, to obviate the delimiting error explicit in, and banality of, choice. In other words, to reify

---

37 Among others, Peter Wollen's general thesis re Warhol's filmic output: see *Andy Warhol: Film Factory*, ibid.

the undeniable. Invariably, anything a maker might add to this world was vulnerable, open to its abstract indefensibility, the tedium of carping, and that excruciating, inescapable carping on the roads not taken. It was one thing to remove himself to the extent of having me write and direct the film, but how did I remove myself then as *my* only way of removing him, my instructor (in both senses)?

The task of the script, a "script" unknown to the actors and in the sense that it required reassembling within the very hour-ten of creating, unknown to me, then, was to prepare a field, to arrange a comfort in which to allow, elicit, or conjole the emergence of the indismissible.

That much settled, the assignment now seemed too great for mere mortals lacking an assist from Providence (see below on the artist's Catholicism). But, sure as the Fiend, such was to come with the first uncourted[38] "intervention": when the elevator doors opened on the fifth-floor Factory and in with its trainer came not a modest and accommodating pony, but Mighty Byrd, a black stallion of staggering dimension—a half-ton of muscle about to confront a noisy crew and crowd, garish overheads and flashing cameras, the *Faust*-blaring phonograph, a woman with an ominous-looking boom aimed right at it, and four altogether dismayed performers. Andy apologized profusely to me for the misunderstanding with Dawn Animal Agency, and true to form when faced with the unexpected, wrung his hands, curled down the corners of his mouth, and chatted nervously. However, it was pointless to dilute, let alone dissipate one's resolve because, as

---

38   The overall semi-disorder of the filming process may obviate calling any error "uncourted." But scholars like Callie Angell argue that all the interventions are intentional "destabilizations." This is seriously inaccurate. Callie Angell, T*he Films of Andy Warhol: Part II* (New York: Whitney Museum Press, 1994).

always until now, his surgical detection would and did proceed.

But then, when Reel One was set to roll, and in the teeth of the stalwart trainer's assurances, that demonic fortuity the gathering to a man held its collective breath against inevitably happened. Unnerved by the above instigation, and because the squatting actors had inadvertently moved in too close, virtually under its belly despite my stage-whispered, frantic admonitions to the contrary, and following Tosh's test-touching of its flank that I intended as a fleeting reference to bestiality, the stallion kicked him in the head and opened a flowing gash his shock prevented him from responding to or even feeling. So that moments later when the stock was unwinding, and I'd cue the other three to accuse Max, played by Tosh—the very handsomest of all the beautiful people attracted to the Factory, and easily the most exotic—of card cheating and to shake him down for his chips, what I saw was that they, unaware, out of control, and perhaps out of suppressed envy, found little resistance in Tosh when they released their fears on him, the victim, in a vicious and sadistic orgy of racist assault. Which mobilized *Horse* and drove that vagabond reeler to its statement on human nature: unsponsored, plenipotent, and indismissible.

John Rockwell claims that Philip Glass came to his signature sound from a misunderstanding of Indian ragas.[39] More, that this is not the first time art was misperception's bounty. Some who watch *Horse* or were even there at its popper-penetrated shoot deny the occurrence of so violent an incision as I witnessed. Some are sure to say that it's precisely my seeing what should have happened but didn't that made necessary a Ridiculous Theatre. To the point as well is that I, circling and periodically intruding into

---

39   John Rockwell, *All American Music: Composition in the Late Twentieth Century* (New York: Knopf, 1983), Philip Glass chapter.

the shot, did experience what I describe, and so reinforced just that, composing the crucifixion image of Tosh and myself that, to the strains (from the record player I'd switched on) of "Anges Pures," closes the film.

Both immaterial to and whatever the case, the transfer and admittance into live event of this particular filmic modality—i.e., that the text function as an underground for the actors through and above which they will articulate themselves in and as the evening's statement—earmarks the early Ridiculous occasion.

The Life of Juanita Castro, the movie I wrote, from-in-the-shot directed, and starred in (as "Cueman" or "Stage Manager"[40]), which was made just prior to *Horse*, casts additional light on this emphasis, although the balance in the dialectic of field or underground and "incisions" is in reverse. For what happens is, the underground is so weighted with political position, from some details of the Cuban revolution aftermath and the scripted deconstruction of political position (altogether) to an ultra-radicalizing of the audience in its radical profilmic deconstruction, that the performed articulate (the "incisions") manages to serve only as compounded layering and energizer for the work's disposition to embarrass that underground with riches. To draft a trope, one partner in the backstreet affair wears the blindfold in *Horse* and the other in *Juanita*.

---

40   As per our procedure for all my shot scripts in 1965, I read the credits aloud onto the track, here at the beginning of the film, in others often piecemeal throughout, and to fill in at slow points. In a safety-net bid (against his probable discomfit) I modestly, almost confusingly, identified myself as "cueman and scenarist." Andrew Sarris was the first to call my acting role in the work "the Stage Manager," after, one supposes, the closest function it recalls in a play. Bearing the same title, a theatre version of this film became my most produced live show piece; characteristic of the silence-conspiracy, Erika Munk, lead critic of *The Village Voice*'s theatre department throughout the '70s and '80s, denied for years ever hearing of such a stage work.

Attempts to decipher someone else's perception are wild conjecturing at best, and how much more so when that perception was as equivocal as Andy's. So I can't say whether, when he studied *The Life of Juanita Castro*, he was disturbed by the prominence given to the modern in it—after we imagine, for example, he imagined he had cleared that hurdle. Or if, checking the results of *Horse*, he was pleased with the phoenixing there of a postmodernism from the rubble of modernity. He considered and categorized an echelon of deconstruction: beyond that, I'm not sure that he reflected on the films in such received terms or in ways any longer open to us. It's certain that the filmwork was somewhat more calculated[41] and as I'm indicating more progressive than previously thought. And when researchers prompt my memory with notes in his hand or clippings that he hoarded, the browsing apothegms that he dictated to me for the Bloomingdale's of his aesthetic keep multiplying.

Significantly, immediately after wrapping *Horse*—to which he nervously affixed a full-reel study of Mighty Byrd at ease— Andy steered me to the writing of "literary" scripts and loose adaptations: *Vinyl*, a take on *Clockwork Orange*, *Kitchen*, an original, *Piano*, a recycled kids' piece of mine, and *Kahuna!* and *Shower*, both originals. The first he incised by preventing the lead, Gerard, from rehearsing, which he called "littering," i.e., the Factory, and then from even learning his lines by sending Gerard out on round-the-clock deliveries. But other than the addition, and introduction, of photogenic Edie Sedgwick, it is almost certain that his were not thoughtful incisions, referred to these days with

---

41   Callie Angell, ibid., ftn. 35, and in research of hers slated for future publication. On the other hand, Warhol's famous remark about the films, "They're better talked about than seen" (in Paul Taylor, "Andy Warhol: the Last Interview," *Flash Art* no. 133, April 1987), must be taken seriously. It strongly suggests that he did not fully understand or appreciate the value of some of the movies that were coming to be under his aegis.

unwarranted patience as "destabilizations," so much as petty deconcentrations. His mind was elsewhere, he being hell-bent on evening some score with Gerard as the latest episode in their up-energy, down-energy interminable feud. The celebrated mid-reel cut to a closeup of Gerard in the leather hood and slow zoom out to the previous (main) frame was the result of the Auricon's breaking down and Buddy Wirtschafter, the cameraman's, repair job. When he told me he could resume filming only with that closeup, I suggested he do so and then pace-zoom to duplicate the movie's opening. Remarkably, *Vinyl* surmounts the disorder of its shoot.

On Andy's order, *Kitchen* was a situation screenplay, and his decision to conventionally co-direct it with me (i.e., Hollywood-style) made obvious from the start his hope to shoot it straight—because he believed he had found his ticket to Tinseltown in the star qualities of Edie Sedgwick. So his discovery of the extent of her drug habit, which rendered that and his Hollywood dreams unfeasible for the moment, proved the society-column team's first real falling-out. And the remaining scripts in this batch, all fashioned as vehicles for her to more or less formally act, fell victim to Edie's drugging and "close friend" drug suppliers as well, and went unshot.

A sentence in *Street of Stairs* reads: "Geography is truth, truth geography." Therefore, I was not unprepared when, in July, Andy leaned toward a "mapping" movie—to be called *Space* (in some filmographies now *Space 1965*). However, beyond not only learning lines at this point but even reading them—our intention for *Space* so as not to tax her temper or capacity—Edie lent an ear to the Morrissey-Wein suggestion that she express bewilderment at the abstract scenario and tear the script up on-camera. Suspecting something was afoot even before the shoot, and caught in the downward spiral, Andy lost his legendary cool and displaced his anger onto the convenient whipping boy by insisting that I remove

Gerard's presence and credits from the work. One of my darkest images of the East Forty-Seventh Street studio is Andy's starting from a considerable distance and clattering across the concrete in his scalloped brown cowboy boots—myself by then kneeling close to the floor set to whisper instructions to performers—to tower above me and seethe his vengeful mandate re the huffing Gerard just then in the Velázquez "Infanta" dramatics of an upstage and upstaged leave-taking via the Factory's clanging door. The footage records the destruction of the script and how pathetic the twelve cast members are at improvising instead.

Not to lose my own time, that September I drafted much of the dialogue intended for *Space* into the Jacob's ladder section of *The Life of Lady Godiva*. As our second Ridiculous presentation (in effect, our third stage piece) *Godiva* premiered in April '66 with no one the wiser for it.

Ondine[42] was fond of retailing Andy's habit of setting up Della-Drellas[43] against each other, in order to keep them in line or enhance his control—in Ondine's version, basically for sadistic curiosity's sake. To quote: "He just wasn't good to his friends." But confused by the triple power-play he had set in motion, and thinking perhaps he'd outsmarted himself, Andy suddenly seemed clean out of creative ideas for me. His next step therefore was to ask if there were any movie that I especially wanted to make myself. Though I decided to keep my own counsel in considering this, for the time being I told him no. It seemed *hors de ligne*

---

42   Stage name of the late Robert Olivo, the Pope of *The Chelsea Girls*. Ondine enjoyed a stage as well as film career. Harvey Tavel directed him in the titular role of a memorable version of *The Life of Juanita Castro* (1971-72).

43   The entourage's not altogether flattering nickname for Andy was Drella, presumably for its witch-like quality. In turn, the entourage itself was called, unsparingly enough, the "Drella-Dellas." (I've seen this misspelled more often than not.)

that projects wholly my own, in concept, development, initiation, writing, rehearsing, directing, etc., should be presented under Warhol's name. And since I'd become involved with perpetuating The Theatre of The Ridiculous by then, directions I came up with myself naturally might be needed for the stage.

But since I also could not predict what art or idea venues The Play-House might withstand, or even how long it would last, given the volatile personalities involved, I decided to develop the next few scripts in formats adaptable to either medium. This is how *Indira Gandhi's Daring Device* came to be written in the fall of '65—as a film or stage vehicle for the darkly exotic Julie Garfield[44], a strong replacement for Raul in the St. Mark's Playhouse run of *The Life of Juanita Castro*. To be sure, by the time *Indira Gandhi* went up, as a stage scandal in September 1966, it starred Jeanne Phillips in the title role: for Ms. Garfield would in no wise entertain doing a "weirdo" Warhol movie and had long since left the Play-House of The Ridiculous itself for Anton Chekhov and other realistic oeuvre she considered her forte.

Some time later (i.e., circa mid-fall '66) Andy, drawn deeper into the morass he'd allowed Edie and her aides to create for him, concluded that I should be reserved for commercial films — to be done under producers' contract, with advances, residuals, et al., that the rewards for either of us systematically extending as we had been the exploration into the nature of film were running out. Under this arrangement, and with Fu Fu Smith representing Huntington Hartford III, I scripted the three-hour *Jane Eyre Bare* — on Andy's speculation, tailoring it for model Baby Jane Holzer.

Notwithstanding the above, in February 1966, having finally managed to extricate himself legally from Chuck Wein, Don Lyons, and Edie, and leaving the latter to fulfill her predictable destiny

---

44 Daughter of John Garfield. She was six when he died. She actually is named for him: his real first name was "Julie."

(four years later she fatally overdosed), Andy got his second wind re screenplay-features — and some fresh inspiration via the Velvet Underground. Idling while the Play-House searched for that new location when he called me, I returned to the Factory and wrote four features that were filmed late that winter and in the summer of '66. These were: *Hedy, or the 14-Year-Old Girl*, a provocation set in motion by Hedy Lamarr's arrest for kleptomania at the time, starring Mario Montez, Harvey Tavel, Mary Woronov, Ingrid Superstar, Jack Smith, and me, scored by the Velvet Underground, with Warhol himself on (moving) camera; *Withering Sights*, an adaptation of the Brontë novel; *Hanoi Hanna, Radio Star* with Mary Woronov's stunning interpretation; and *Their Town*, a reflection on Wilder's *Our Town* with the sympathetic mise-en-scène of Billy Name and a restrained, touching performance by Eric Emerson.

In 1970 the *Hanoi Hanna* script was elaborated into a linguistically complex commentary on the Vietnam war (retitled *Vinyl Visits an FM Station*) at the request of producers Albee-Barr-Wilder and handsomely mounted as the final offering at the Playwrights' Unit, their Off-Off-Broadway house. And shortly afterwards a Los Angeles production of this stage piece aired on California Public TV.

Their Town's dazzling color kaleidoscope and serial-killer theme were clearly seminal to Andy's human skull, red and green self-portrait, and other eschatological color studies. The script itself was developed (in 1969-71) into a musical, *Boy on the Straight-Back Chair*, the work for which I received more awards than any other, and which nowadays commonly is referred to as the study that launched the serial-killer genre.

Hanoi Hanna, Radio Star and *Their Town* are my two most frequently screened efforts since, although originally shown independently, they more familiarly survive as sequences in *The Chelsea Girls*.

My remaining days on Forty-Seventh Street produced more pieces in dialogue that were never shot, among them *Lucrezia Borgia's Catered Affair, Luncheonette*, and *Movie Talk for Mary Woronov*. I worked on *Jail* extempore (much as over two years earlier on *Bitch*), handicapped this time by only a passing familiarity with most of the actors.

I left the Factory to concentrate on theatrical presentations with a half-dozen filmscripts suitable for staging with little change, a half-dozen suitable if one cared to put more effort into them, and a lifetime's worth of pondering on the dichotomy of human nature as the legacy of a man who could so surmount his culture as to become the Father of (Its) Deconstruction, and on the other hand be so much the slave of its least admirable features as to encourage a collaborator to deny ever having met him without blinking.

With the exception of college tours, the Ridiculous events almost always were presented in relatively confined settings. Since the audience could follow the performers' intimately mutable features, their evolving and dissolving thoughts, the use of characters, as in the scripted films, as hatcheries in which to process the performers' "characterizing" themselves was automatic. And after studying the dramatic fiat, i.e., how people invent (and define) a self before and for onlookers, I wrote a further set of pieces upping the complexity of the scripted characters so that trained Ridiculous personalities could engage in vigorous *inter*-plays between the live person they were evolving for us and their fictional front, often nominally, and paradoxically, live public persons, i.e., selves elsewhere invented, of prominence.

If one makes the case that before the rigor mortis kiss of American neo-naturalism, historically theatre always functioned somewhat resembling the above, Ridiculous occasions differed in that they formally insisted on our attention to function, and thus all stand in and up to the process of categorizing historical and naturalistic stagework. The personal note in (or what makes) Ridiculous deconstruction is the pro- and joyful democratic leveling of animal, plant, and human life, and high and low culture: identified by the persistent Ridiculous reminders, among other communications, of the filmworld from which these occasions derive — not just the cutting edge of underground work, but of the Hollywood patrimony itself in which moviemakers from Warhol and Brakhage to Smith, Ken Jacobs, and the Kuchars saw themselves included. So that *The Life of Lady Godiva* recalls along with Genesis, its source, *Lady Godiva of Coventry* (with George Nader and Maureen O'Hara, Universal-International, 1953); while *Arenas of Lutetia* ghosts *Siren of Atlantis* (United Artists, 1947), its model; and *Gorilla Queen* lets hardly a half-dozen lines go by without citing instance, attitude, or predicaments of Hollywood exotica, from its main inspiration, *Captive Wild Woman* (John Carradine and Acquanetta, Republic, 1943) to *Four Brave Souls* (Paramount, 1938), *Down Argentine Way* (Fox, 1040), *Tangier* (Universal, 1946), and, of course, *King Kong* (Radio Pictures, 1933).[45]

In their epiphanic, countercultural moment, as in *Horse*, seminal to them, these "plays" are plenipotentiary.

---

45 Acquanetta (a k a Mildred Davenport, b. 1921 in Wyoming), nicknamed the "Venezuelan Volcano." Her major vehicle, *Captive Wild Woman*, and its sequel, *Jungle Woman*, are the secret ingredients in *Gorilla Queen*—though I tried to draw attention to the lady by making her a lead character in *Notorious Harik Will Kill the Pope*. She apparently is alive and well in Arizona, and may merely have been filling Republic's need for an exotic-looking sarong girl during World War II, but those films dealt with transmogrification and scared the living daylights out of me as a child. People have told me *Gorilla Queen* similarly haunts them. Leslie Fiedler may have stumbled upon the reasons for the threat in this material: see his *Freaks: Myths and Images of the Secret Self* (New York: Simon & Schuster, 1978). For my own unpublished work, like *Harik*, see the Ronald Tavel Collection, Mugar Memorial Library, Boston University, 771 Commonwealth Avenue, Boston.

III
Strange Tyranny

In *Byron and Shakespeare*, G. Wilson Knight claims that the romantic poet is the archetypical romantic precisely because he has one foot in the Nineteenth Century, and the other pointedly in the Eighteenth.[46]

One hears now and with increasing enlistment that Andy Warhol is the archetypical (and foremost) artist of the second half of our century because he is the quintessential postmodern. But what makes one that?

We know, of course, that Andy accompanied his incapacitated mother to Sunday Mass, that he continued attending alone after her death but as if in her quite living company, and that he himself is buried in hallowed ground. Some who would reinvent him for theoretical purposes dismiss the first activity as mere filial obligation, the second as an artist's "weirdness," and the last as insignificant protocol. But if you gather the omnipresent religious iconography of the films, the film Imitation of Christ, the numerous studies in Eschatology — the Skull series, the Execution series, the "Living" Death Mask series, and the film *Suicide*[47] among others — and add them to his renderings of the Last Supper with their size, severity, and serenity, it would seem indefensible to claim that you've not the consistency in output here of a devout Catholic. And then, in the last fifteen years of his life, in such work as the Chairman Mao and Endangered Animal series, the Single-Marilyns, the Mick Jaggers, the Hand-to-Face Self-Portraits and other large portraits, Warhol stepped forward as a major colorist. A primary colorist, certainly, but the stress

---

46 G. Wilson Knight, *Byron and Shakespeare* (London: Routledge & Kegan Paul, 1966).

47 *Suicide* was the Factory's first color feature. I think it is easily one of the best films that I did for Andy. It is unique. It never was released.

is on beauty in the most conventional reading of painterly beauty — in this respect he achieves a standing on a par with Matisse. Now, consider the treasury of his heavily early but nonetheless lifelong contribution to the history of exquisite sketching, and I think we've enough credentials amassed to qualify this artist as a High Modern. —Or more, that in the case of his card-carrying membership in a formal, "objective" religion, we may be dealing with a shortcoming that invalidates a place for him even among the most pristine moderns.

Might not readings along these lines also describe Beckett, so off-handedly called nowadays literature's classic postmodern? If the principal body of Genet's work, and especially Kafka's, makes them moderns, what in Beckett's prolific metaphysics isn't measuring up—even to Joyce's or Adorno's lofty expectations, intent on honoring Aristotle? But is this, as if in a neat parallel to Byron, a taprooting with the moderns in order to bloom the more essentially as a postmodern—or are both these categories (especially, as agonistic) inadequate?

We live with a strange tyranny of theory when the reiterated division, evidently oppositional, of the modern and postmodern gains such currency as to have the cowed lion's share of educators concerned dutifully stuck in these term tar-pits. If that breakdown works for Madonna and Loni Anderson, does it apply to Meredith Monk, Roy Orbison, Randy Newman, or Tom Waits? If the entropy of Pynchon fills the bill, do the socio-political cosmologies of William Burroughs, Pier Paolo Pasolini, Eric Rohmer, Wong Kar-Wai, John McNaughton, or Derek Jarman? There is a time-honored tradition in criticism of ignoring the aspects of an artist that don't fit comfortably into the era theory of that artist. Artists not fitting the theory at all are conveniently overlooked.

In addition, unexpected innovators like Burroughs, De Sade,

Wu Bin[48], and Mae West, for instance, who can't be poured into the prevailing politically correct molds, never make the canon — which needs noting since a glance at (published) *theatre* theory shows that only commercially promoted and canonically sanctioned samplings (and, suspiciously, Broadway pap) receive serious quarterlies' recognition. We should not have to point out that by substituting sentimentality and sympathy for compassion, political correctness becomes the good taste of thought: because good taste, to repeat Andrew Sarris, is the most insidious enemy of the avant garde. But then again, who pass for the alert today are going to insist that now there can be no avant garde (meaning, actual art) anyhow. And because studies in real new art must always confront dilemmas of difficulty and rebellion, theirs make a stab at being — with the aid of theory-illustrator artist (sic), victim-artist (sic), and silent, disaffected professorial conspiracy — self-fulfilling prophecies.

In America today Performance has replaced theatre because an event or occasion in or as proposal presents a world actually, and paradoxically, too coherent as well perhaps for a posteducated public. Muddying the waters, actors, confused in their own minds with their iconic nature (possibly because many of The Ridiculous actors have been nearly as "demented" as their roles), have trouble understanding, along with stage historians, how much of the commentary on their character in the later Ridiculous scripts in particular is already incorporated into the text: and that this requires them either to back off entirely or start off where the script leaves off.

---

48   A late Ming Dynasty painter prominent in the suppressed, and all but written out of history, Qi movement (pronounced Chi, meaning "strange"). Its followers advocated an independence from Confucian culture, extreme behavior, and self-truth. See *The Landscapes of Wu Bin* (c. 1543-c. 1626) and "A 17th-Century Discourse of Originality" by Katharine Persis Burnette (dissertation, University of Michigan, Ann Arbor, 1995).

If the wholesale deconstruction of all binary oppositeness is *Gorilla Queen* and its two dozen companion aggressions a full quarter-century before such was called for in theoretical circles, and the tracts' celebratory attitude toward anomie in general puzzled and antagonized the vested critical interest until quite recently (and in all but the most progressive college environments still do), should that same interest also go unquestioned for its continuing insensitivity to their decentering of the deathly cultural norms and faiths, of film, stage, and state, snug and smug in their barricaded lease of manufactured feeling? Or to what Michael Smith in *Contemporary Dramatists*[49] termed "the turning of [their] formidable energy to the service of a passion for justice"?

---

49 *Contemporary Dramatists*, 4th Edition (Chicago and London: St. James Press, 1988).

INDEX OF NAMES AND TITLES

John McNaughton, 164
Don McNeill, 142f
Taylor Mead, 80
A Medal for Benny, 109
Jonas Mekas, 44, 125
Marie Menken, 34, *35*, 38-41, 126
Ismail Merchant, 112
Peter Michelson, 141f
Mighty Byrd, 45, *45*, 152, 155
Deborah Miller, 150f
J. J. Mitchell, 72
Meredith Monk, 163
Maria Montez, xii-xiv, xvii, 4, 22,
    138f
Mario Montez (René Rivera), xv, 4,
    5, 20-26, 27, 34, 81, 89, 91-95, 112,
    138, 159
Michael Moon, 25
Sterling Morrison, 86
Paul Morrissey, 25, 69, 80, 92, 115,
    156
Movie Talk for Mary Woronov, xv,
    117-119, 160
Erika Munk, 154f
Tom Murrin, 139f
My Foetus Lived on Amboy Street,
    74-75, 79, 106, 144f, 147
My Hustler, 78
My Little Chickadee, 46
George Nader, 161
Billy Name (Billy Linich), x, 3, 44-
    46, 53, 109-110, 114-115, 136, 150f,
    159
Ogden Nash, 11
Randy Newman, 163
Mme. Ngo Ding Nhu, 107
Nico, 74, 87, 112
Nightmare Alley, 25
Normal Love, xix
Notorious Harik Will Kill the Pope,
    79, 144f, 161f
Notre Dame de Paris, 20, 25, 81
Rudolf Nureyev, 10

The Nutcracker in the Land of Nuts,
    132f, 144f
Merle Oberon, 98
The Off-Off-Broadway Book, 132f
Maureen O'Hara, 161
Ondine (Robert Olivo), 43, 48-49, *50*,
    78. 98, 107, 112, 118, 120, 123-124,
    127, 157
Michael O'Pray, 136f
Roy Orbison, 163
Peter Orlovsky, 1
Orphée, 4
Mercedes Ospina, 32, *35*
Our Lady of Paris, 81
Our Town, 116, 159
P. D. Ouspensky, 67
The Ovens of Anita Orangejuice,
    144f
Rochelle Owens, 1
Camille Paglia, 10
Pier Paolo Pasolini, 164
Lester Persky, 39
Jeanne Phillips, 158
Piano, 82, 155
Walter Pidgeon, 85, 94
Alan Plantz, 1
Albert Poland, 132f
Brigid Polk, 112
Poor Little Rich Girl, xiv, 79
Emily Post, 94
Jacques Potin, *50*
Tyrone Power, 25
Thomas Pynchon, 163
Ishmael Reed, 1
Lou Reed, 86-87
Debbie Reynolds, 111
Dusty Rhodes, 78
René Ricard, 10, *55*, 56, 99
*Rock 'n' Roll High School, Parts I
    and II*, 119
John Rockwell, 153
Arnold Rockwood, xv
Rotten Rita, 43

170

171

www.ingramcontent.com/pod-product-compliance
Lightning Source LLC
Chambersburg PA
CBHW072136170526
45158CB00004BA/1394